Fre

to Lead

Freedom to Lead

healthy leaders grow healthy churches

Colin Buckland

First published 2001 as *Liberated to Lead* by Kingsway Publications.
This revised version published 2006, by CWR, Waverley Abbey House, Waverley Lane, Farnham, Surrey GU9 8EP, England

See back of book for list of National Distributors.
Names have been changed to protect the identity of individuals.

Front cover image: Getty/Taxi
Concept development, editing, design and production by CWR.

Printed in Finland by WS Bookwell.

ISBN-13: 978-1-85345-382-3
ISBN-10: 1-85345-382-X

This book is dedicated to my loving wife, Lorna,
who has walked every step of the ministry journey alongside me
as my friend and advisor, and also to Sidney and Gladys Draayer,
mentors and faithful friends, with love.

Contents

Introduction 9

1. Self-awareness and Your Ministry 13
2. Journal Writing in the Ministry 32
3. The Call to Ministry 39
4. Expectation and the Ministry 51
5. Power, Authority and the Ministry 73
6. Family Life and the Pressures of Ministry 91
7. Sexuality and the Ministry 103
8. Ministry and the Devotional Life 126
9. Recognising Burnout in the Ministry 144
10. Overcoming Ministry Burnout 174

Conclusion 201

Resources 203

Notes 204

Introduction

This is a book for all Christian leaders regardless of the type of church, denomination or organisation they belong to. It is strongly based on my course 'Liberating the Leadership', offered originally as a correspondence course through the Open Theological College scheme and now as a distance learning course through the London School of Theology. This book is offered as what we might call 'sanctified common sense' – a realistic and earthy view of ministry life written by an experienced minister and leader who has helped hundreds of Christian leaders around the world find new levels of leadership health and effectiveness.

The need for good leadership exists for the Church today, when many leaders find themselves struggling with the nature of their role. The heart is willing, but sometimes the mind and the body are shouting out a warning as leaders attempt to do the impossible. Doing the impossible is a divine attribute and best left to God while Christian leaders content themselves with doing their best and being their best for His glory. Perhaps one of the biggest needs for the Christian leader is to find out what he or she could or should be attempting. This book points to a new leadership lifestyle; a healthy way of living and serving God and His Church.

The book takes no particular theological stance and isn't offered to a particular Christian readership, other than to leaders who live and work in this role within the Church at large. It includes a few Bible references but assumes that the reader has informed views and belief systems as a leader. It sets out to challenge readers positively to take a journey of personal growth that will enable them to establish new patterns of ministry health as a 'lifestyle' for the future.

Terms such as 'Christian leader', 'minister', 'pastor', or 'vicar' used in this book are interchangeable and are all used to depict the Christian who works as a leader of the local church or in a similar role. I have used them indiscriminately to give an inclusive feel.

Christian leaders are highly pressured. Many will recognise that they are tired and could do with a break, but considerably fewer will recognise the extent to which they are depleted. The rate of burnout and stress breakdown among Christian leaders is exceptionally high, this occupation being listed among the most stressful. Our research in the UK has shown that 28 per cent of all Protestant clergy are seriously considering giving up their calling, as many feel that the expectations of the role far exceed what they imagined their task would be. Many also feel that the role they fulfil is but a shadow of what they responded to as a call to the ministry.

As with any role there is a continuum of experience from elation to depression, but there exists a huge central group who are discouraged with their lot in the Church and feel that their position is a poor representation of how they imagine it should or could be. Many believe they are taking one step forward and two back; that they are getting nowhere with maximum effort.

This is a book about Christian leadership. It's about freedom and personal growth in the ministry; about learning to enjoy serving the Lord and allowing Him to breathe His creative Spirit into His Church in such a way that a greater harvest of fruit is gained by all.

The book will take you through the following areas:

1. Gaining an introduction to self-awareness skills.
2. Learning and practising journalling skills.
3. Considering the nature of 'calling' to Christian service and clarifying the issues.
4. Examining the place of 'expectations' in ministry and in life generally.
5. Examining the issues of power and authority in ministry roles.
6. Considering family life and the pressures of ministry.
7. Exploring some of the issues surrounding sexuality and ministry.
8. Reflecting on the devotional life.
9. Examining the condition called 'burnout'.
10. Demonstrating how to recover from or avoid burnout.

It is designed in such a way that you may read the discussion and participate in a few related exercises, as you wish, that may help you as a leader to develop greater levels of freedom and liberty in your life and Christian service.

Note

The research informing this book was undertaken in two phases under the project name 'Leaders Under Pressure'. Each phase involved gathering similar material but making use of slightly differing methods; namely, person-to-person interviews and postal surveys. The first phase was a person-to-person interview stage completed in 1990. The sample was one hundred serving clergy taken from most of the denominations and church types in the Protestant Church. The sample was taken from ten geographical regions in England researched by MARC Europe (a European research department of World Vision which is a Christian initiative to serve the poor and needy in over forty countries worldwide) to give coverage for the whole of England. Each location name represents a wider area from which the interviewees were drawn.

The interviews were conducted by Keith Roberts, who was a Baptist minister at the time of the survey, serving in a city-based south London church, and Colin Buckland, who between them carried out 95 detailed interviews of the proposed 100. The second phase of the research was constructed and carried out for Keith Roberts and Colin Buckland by MARC Europe and comprised a postal survey sent to approximately 3,000 serving clergymen. A total of 1,020 questionnaires, comprising 34 per cent of the targeted sample, was returned.[1]

1. Self-awareness and Your Ministry

Case study

Graham Cartwright was the grandson of a Congregational minister, George Cartwright, who had been quite well known in his locality. As a child Graham would go to church and listen to his grandfather with a feeling of awe and excitement. This was his grandad and everyone was listening to him and gazing at him with their faces beaming with delight. Often, other churches and groups of churches would invite George to speak. He had an attractive style for that time, which was before television had become the megabusiness it is today, and his preaching drew good-sized crowds. People enjoyed hearing George and always, as they left the building, the congregation talked excitedly about the sermon. But his number one fan was Graham, who basked not only in his grandfather's skills but in the glow of his prestige.

As a boy of ten, Graham had already decided that he too would be a preacher! He would fill the churches just like Grandfather – maybe more so – if he really worked hard at it. He also would have crowds coming to hear him and would enjoy the warmth of their appreciation.

Through the next few years Graham worked hard at school and excelled in the sciences. He seemed to have a natural aptitude for them, and teaching staff vigorously encouraged him to aim for a good university degree and a career in science. Graham enjoyed their attention but was still fixed on following in his grandfather's wake. He was going to be a preacher and that was that.

So, after his secondary education he gained an honours degree in theology at university, followed by a further three years in studying for a master's degree and training for the ministry. During his university years, his grandfather died and the family, along with those few who could still remember George as a skilful preacher, mourned his passing. During his university and ministry training years Graham had been out of contact with his grandfather for much of the time and had not heard him preach for some years. He had gone on to take up the role of minister in a church and hadn't thought too much about the old man's popularity as he was deeply involved in ministry life and little else filled his waking moments.

Graham eventually married and soon he and his wife Jenny started a family. They were excited about family life but Jenny grew increasingly unhappy about Graham's absence from home. It seemed that the family needs grew with time and Graham's church involvement was just the same as when they first married. He had not adjusted his workload with the arrival of either of their two children and, if anything, seemed to be working harder with every passing year.

Graham struggled with ministry life and found that after the first eighteen months in the pastorate he started to become unpopular. Church members began saying that he was not a good listener and that his sermons were difficult to understand. This caused Graham to panic and all he could think about was working harder. He visited more people each week and spent longer preparing his sermons, but the net result was that he had less time for visitation and the criticism of him increased.

Time passed and Graham's stress levels ballooned until he had to take time off through ill health, a thing he hated to do. He was physically, mentally and spiritually low, and felt he had been let down. His wife was unhappy with him and their relationship was strained. He had worked hard for the church, but no amount of work seemed to improve his popularity. The congregation was shrinking and he felt that God had let him down. He believed that God had heard him pledge to be a preacher when he was just a boy and he had worked hard for God on his education and ministry preparation. What more could he do?

Following the encouragement of a respected friend in the ministry, Graham went for counselling. Here, through an exercise in self-awareness, he realised he had been driven to succeed by his desire to be as popular as his grandfather had been. His own father had spent little time with him in a healthy father–son relationship, since he too was a popular local preacher and was always out preaching. Popularity that leads to a lack of healthy family dynamics costs dear. Graham had not given much thought to the subjects of calling and gifting; he was too busy searching for acceptance. He was good at studying and was an academic but lacked interpersonal skills and his preaching style was dull and too complex for Sunday sermons. His family had suffered from his absence as he strove to become what he essentially was not.

Graham learned that he had mistaken his need to be needed and to be popular as a call to the ministry and had bound himself as a child to a role he was unable to fulfil. For the next months his task was to find out who he really was and what he enjoyed doing. What energised and motivated him? Through his journey of self-awareness he realised that God had not let him down at all but that he had followed the wrong path and for the wrong reasons. Graham, now a university lecturer, is happier than he has ever been. His wife Jenny and their three children enthusiastically echo this.

I like a story with a happy ending but am convinced that we need not always learn our biggest lessons in life through suffering. Who and what am I? This is the essence of self-awareness. I believe we can avoid pain, wasted time, mistaken journeys and the passing of fruitless years through the journey of self-awareness. One of the greatest, most beneficial discoveries you will ever make will be the discovery of *you*.

This is a subject requiring a good measure of honesty if anyone wishes to make the best use of such a journey. Living in a busy world that seemingly requires us to perform to our 'best' may often mean that we have little or no chance to reflect on self-awareness. Most commonly we are able to be self-critical or self-doubting, but true self-awareness may not be on the agenda. I am convinced that the skills of self-awareness provide us with a learning curve that can lead to increased personal freedom, a deepening spiritual life and the ability to be more in control of our lives. I feel like a double-glazing salesman making these statements, as if I need to convince you to take your 'journey of a lifetime'. There should be little point in my selling this to anyone, since personal motivation is the key to establishing and maintaining health in ministry.

Growing to be more self-aware requires a measure of stillness and the courage to begin the journey of self-reflection.

The inner journey

Permission

Most of us will probably lack self-awareness at times and be preoccupied or out of touch because of the pace of life. This may have much to do with our general approach to life. Self-awareness can be an embarrassing topic and we may take offence if the suggestion is made that we are not fully self-aware. In truth most of us are not as self-aware as we could be, but once we have passed any embarrassment barriers, becoming more self-aware is a liberating dynamic. Focusing on self-awareness can be a new experience for many of us.

It can be quite confusing to know whether self-awareness is somehow linked with self-absorption, and thus sin. Many people lack the freedom to explore their inner self and Christians, as they go through their lives, are often urged to become increasingly aware of others and less aware of themselves.

Consider this prayer from the sixteenth century:

> Teach us, good Lord, to serve thee as thou deservest; to give and not to count the cost; to fight and not to heed the wounds; to toil and not to ask for rest; to labour and not to ask for any reward save knowing that we do thy will. Through Jesus Christ our Lord. (Ignatius of Loyola)

These are admirable sentiments expressed in a famous prayer loved by many. It suggests the putting down of personal needs in favour of the needs of others, which is an attitude of Christian selflessness. But good though this may be, it may muddy the issue for some, since self-awareness has been misunderstood as 'selfishness'. The Christian dynamic of self-sacrifice often causes Christians to miss out on the joy of learning about themselves. For some, and this would include Christian leaders, any focus on self is an act of self-interest and therefore selfish and contrary to the Christian spirit. Self-awareness has been relegated to the realm of unhelpful navel-gazing.

I want to draw a distinction between selfishness (or self-centredness) and self-awareness, and so I present the following definitions: *Selfishness* is a heart/mind attitude based solely on gratifying a person's own wants and needs. *Self-awareness* is a heart/mind attitude based on growth and learning so that the individual may function and feel better in all walks of life, work and service.

This book aims, in part, to help you to increase your self-awareness and the skills that lead to it. But you must first give yourself permission to make the journey. As Matthew Arnold said in *Self Dependence*: 'Resolve to be thyself; and know that he who finds himself loses his misery.'

Self-love

Not only do I believe that self-awareness is a helpful and necessary tool, but I believe that self-love can be understood as an act of worship:

> One of the teachers of the law came and heard them debating. Noticing that Jesus had given them a good answer, he asked him, 'Of all the commandments, which is the most important?'
> 'The most important one,' answered Jesus, 'is this: "Hear, O Israel, the Lord our God, the Lord is one. Love the Lord your God with all your heart and with all your soul and with all your mind and with all your strength." The second is this: "Love your neighbour as yourself." There is no commandment greater than these.' (Mark 12:28–31)

These few verses focus on the central biblical theme of love, emphasising that the most important thing in life is to love God. From this dynamic all the rest of life flows. But secondly we are to love others (our 'neighbours' are not simply the family next door, by the way) as we *love ourselves*. To my mind, I cannot begin to know how to love my neighbours if I don't know how to love myself. It would seem that to love my self, then, is to be obedient to Jesus' teaching and essential in the whole process of loving others.

In my efforts to please God, I have to find out what is so lovable about me. The secret behind self-love is not to confuse it with selfishness, but to see it as the recognition of that miracle of creation that has resulted in me.

> For you created my inmost being; you knit me together in my mother's womb. I praise you because I am fearfully and wonderfully made; your works are wonderful, I know that full well. My frame was not hidden from you when I was made in the secret place. When I was woven together in the depths of the earth, your eyes saw my unformed body. All the days ordained for me were written in your book before one of them came to be. (Psa. 139:13–16)

The psalmist uses language beautifully when he tells God that he has recognised His handiwork in creating him. It is intimate language that spells out God's plan and part in bringing him into this world: 'Before I formed you in the womb I knew you, before you were born I set you apart' (Jer. 1:5). I am aware that this is about Jeremiah, but God has no favourites and this, together with the passage from Psalm 139, points to human birth as an important event in the divine calendar. It is heart-warming to think that God takes so much interest in us all. We are each unique in all time: there is only one you! There will never be another you! God knew exactly what He was doing when He made you. It's as if the whole of His plan is like a jigsaw puzzle and we are all individual pieces. There is a you-shaped space in the heart, mind and plan of God that no one else can fill!

If this is true, and the Bible seems to suggest it is, then God has invested a great deal in making you and me. Self-awareness and self-love are about discovering and appreciating what God has done in creating the uniqueness and giftedness of this one human being. To grasp the wonder of my making helps me to be in touch with the value of human life and therefore the value of other human lives. It increases my level of appreciation of myself and others. To acknowledge God's handiwork, then, is an act of worship. I have had the privilege of being able to share these perspectives with a number of Christian leaders in different parts of the world through retreats and seminars and, simple though these thoughts may be, the listeners have been deeply impacted as they have reflected on their own importance to God.

Fear

One of the thieves of personal freedom is fear. An enemy of self-awareness, fear raises its ugly head as a brake on journeying into our unknown. Some people have grown up with a low level of self-worth and are afraid to grow in self-awareness, because they believe that their worst fears will be confirmed. They are afraid that they will learn that they are useless, stupid, ugly and a host of other negative expressions of low self-esteem. In my experience, of those whom I have encouraged to go this way, all have found out that they were not as awful as they believed, and have benefited from the journey.

Another aspect of this is the fear of the unknown, not related to self-esteem but to the fear of new things or changes. We may think that the safest thing to do is to remain as we are and to allow nothing to change around us. In truth, this is really a failure to acknowledge that nothing stays the same; everything is changing – we just choose not to perceive it.

Once again, in my experience those who conquer their fears and journey inwards are not disappointed. As James Thurber said: 'Let us not look back in anger, nor forward in fear, but around in awareness.'

Faith

The Christian journey of self-awareness is a journey that could be said to have two directions: selfwards and Godwards. The more we discover how God has made us, the more we see of Him. It's a little like the creation being a form of God's self-revelation; we see Him in it all, we learn more of Him as a by-product of our journey of self-discovery.

The journey begins

This next section provides the reader with encouragement and simple tools to take the next steps towards increased self-awareness.

Charting the past

On page 20 is a simple diagram to help you chart something of your life through the years. Plot horizontally the years at a rate of two to five years to each block. Plot vertically how positive or negative an event it was that you are charting. Look at the examples below:

1. Simple lifeline – years or blocks of years of your life from birth to date, in whatever detail you may need.
2. Spiritual lifeline – you could use another colour on the same graph and plot the events of your spiritual life in the same way and compare the relationship between your life and your spiritual journey.

This is a simple reflective tool to help you get in touch with some of the significant events in your life and how they have impacted you. Once you have completed this, think how these events have changed you or shaped your future from that point on.

The Lifeline

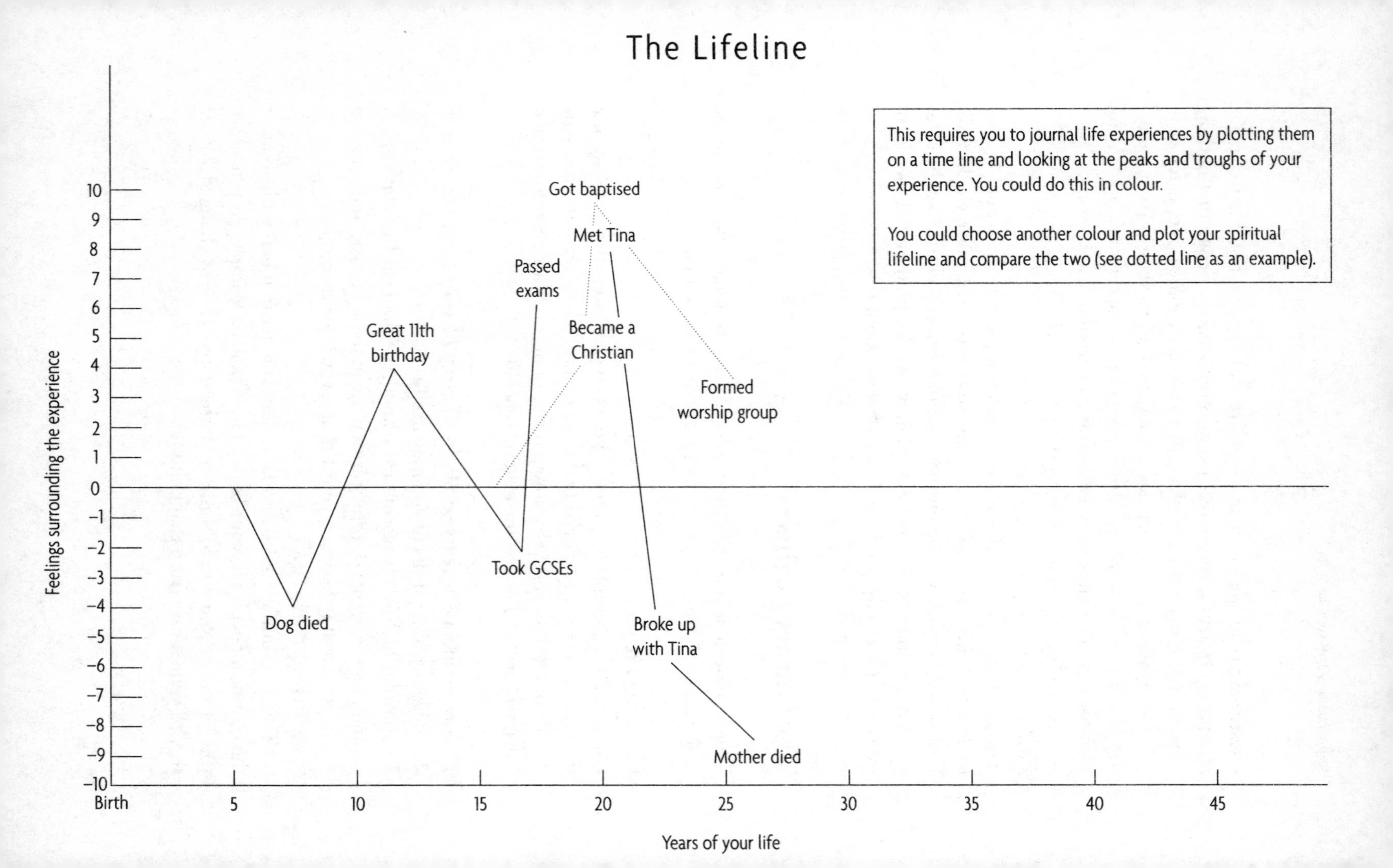

Personal profiling

The following is an exercise in recording personal details as a reflection on what you know about yourself. Just copy these details down on a piece of paper. If you can't answer some, record the fact on your paper.

- Where and when were you born?
- Draw a simple family tree going back as far as you can remember. (Reflect on any emerging feelings as you do this.)
- Spend a little time reflecting on your family tree.
- Write down two unpleasant things you can remember from childhood. (For instance, 'I got the measles' or 'My hamster died', etc. For some of us there will be quite a number of things and some of magnitude. Only do this if you feel comfortable about it.)
- Write down four positive things you can remember from your childhood.
- What is your:
  - favourite colour?
  - favourite food?
  - favourite music?
- Who is your
  - favourite person and why?
  - favourite person from history and why?
- Write down the ten worst things about yourself.
- Write down the ten best things about yourself. (Often harder to do.)
- Write down the ten most significant achievements you recall from your life.
- Now describe your personality in not more than forty words.
- Reflect on the data gathered and endeavour to acknowledge on paper what feelings have surfaced as you have completed this section and how it has made you feel overall.

Learning to reflect

We live in a busy world that offers little stillness, and yet the Bible says: 'Be still, and know that I am God' (Psa. 46:10). William Cowper said: 'A life all turbulence and noise may seem to him that leads it wise and to be praised, but wisdom is a pearl with most success sought in still waters' (*The Task, Book III*). Lao Tse (Chinese philosopher, fifth century BC) said: 'Muddy water let stand, becomes clear.'

Each of these sayings points to a much-needed truth: stillness is a missing commodity in modern life. With its loss much peace, observation and joy of living has gone, and in its place has come the age of stress. To reflect is simply to be quiet, while giving the focus of your reflection a chance to speak to you. Andrew Brandon once said: 'Read the silence that speaks.' Although it sounds mystical, it isn't. It's just recovering an age-old ability to tune in to God and all that He has made, including our inner being.

John Greenleaf Whittier put it this way: 'Drop thy still dews of quietness till all our strivings cease; take from our souls the strain and stress, and let our ordered lives confess the beauty of thy peace.'

Stopping to reflect is to engage powers of observation that are lost in the rush of life. The quality of life is negatively affected by the omission of important things such as beauty, peace and tranquillity. Reflection can mean recovery. Throughout this book, and as a philosophical part of its teaching on leadership health, you will be encouraged to reflect on thoughts and feelings that emerge for you. This is part of the 'awareness' dynamic.

Reflection

Reflecting is being still – purposefully! Find a quiet place and reflect for ten minutes. Focus on what you can hear, see and smell. Reactivate your awareness and your ability to listen. Describe your experience on a separate piece of paper or in a journal.

Understanding and dealing with feelings

Human beings are complex, and I am sure you are well aware of that fact. It is interesting when talking about feelings to recognise that our feelings or emotions have a source and that they operate on a cause-and-effect continuum. Our minds, bodies and nervous systems are linked in such a way that at the level of our emotions we may be changed physically by what we think.

For example: a person afraid of dogs in adult life will feel the physical and emotional symptoms of fear and sometimes panic upon coming into close contact with a dog. Is this because there is certain knowledge that the dog will attack, or certain knowledge that all dogs are dangerous? No, it is based on a recording in the mind that dogs are dangerous, planted there either by an experience of a dangerous dog or a second-hand fear lodged in a person's mind by someone suggesting that dogs are dangerous. The dog may intend to plant a slobbering wet lick on your exposed flesh as a friendly hello, but you see only teeth, gums and mortal danger.

What we feel and why we feel it is often based on previous experience or on information that has impacted our inner being. Translating this to ministry or leadership reminds me of the minister who came to see me because he found that he became uncontrollably emotional when taking the annual Remembrance Day services. Some simple questions revealed that his own father had died as the result of injuries sustained during the Second World War. Unbeknown to this minister, he was simply reacting to unresolved emotions connected to the loss of his father each time Remembrance Day came around. He was remembering, but his memories were connected to inner pain.

This process works at several levels. We may respond to people not so much out of a direct link with what they say so much as to what feelings are triggered as they speak.

Case study

Roger Bryant is a Baptist minister who found throughout his fifteen years' service in three different churches that he could not cope with opposition. He could hardly believe that in all the time he had been a minister he had regularly been opposed to the point where he could no longer continue as minister in each of the churches. He would withstand the opposition for a time but would then have to move to another pastorate.

He came to me as the result of struggling with this opposition in his third pastorate, asking if this was 'spiritual warfare' or some other dynamic. Roger had lacked confidence as a child and, while his parents were very loving, they expected him to do well in his exams to the extent that an 80 per cent pass led to the comment, 'What happened to the other 20?' He never felt that he ever did well enough.

As an adult, Roger had come to interpret all differing views as a personal attack. He could not live comfortably with a leadership team that wanted to evaluate decisions by questioning his viewpoint. This was personal for Roger and it usually blew up out of all proportion. Opposing thoughts appeared to be accusations of failure. His perfectionist tendency had damaged his interpersonal skills, making it difficult for him to work well with a team.

This is not an uncommon example. Roger demonstrates how past experiences may inhabit the present through irrational responses to stimuli. Without making this discovery, Roger could have gone on through his ministry with a victim mentality, probably going from church to church, sure in the knowledge that people were out to get him and pull him down.

Feelings often lead to actions and responses. Emotions are linked with motivation and our response to circumstances. To know 'why I feel what I feel' enables the individual to respond from a place of knowledge and emotional maturity rather than the more common immediate reaction to a series of untapped feelings. We are frequently encouraged into various responses and actions by our feelings and inner recordings from the past. The root of our motivation for action often lies in our feelings.

Emotional maturity

> Do not conform any longer to the pattern of this world, but be transformed by the renewing of your mind. Then you will be able to test and approve what God's will is – his good, pleasing and perfect will. (Rom. 12:2)

> For God did not give us a spirit of timidity, but a spirit of power, of love and of self-discipline. (2 Tim. 1:7)

These passages speak to me not so much of sanity as of peace and balance: that our minds may be renewed by our life with God and that He has given us the opportunity to put down our fears (timidity) and find balanced life and peace (self-discipline, a sound mind, self-control).

This begins to clothe for me what I understand by the expression 'emotional maturity'. Christian leaders will be greatly enabled in their role through a process of personal growth that leads to increased levels of emotional maturity; to be able to make decisions based more in the reality of the moment than from a complexity of emotional responses that colour decisions. Christian leadership has frequently been marred by the emotions-driven 'spiritual ventriloquism' that puts words in the mouth of God that in reality reflect the needs, hopes and wishes of the Christian leader. Many leadership decisions and directions are grounded in motivation sourced by emotions.

Self-awareness, then, includes growth in emotional maturity. Emotional maturity is a deeply personal dynamic, but may be *loosely* defined as:

- Being able to feel comfortable about ourselves (not suggesting that we have reached human perfection but not ill at ease with self)
- Being able to interact well with others with developed social skills (to be with others in such a way that our own performance is not the centre of our attention)
- Being able to meet life's demands with its ups and downs without losing control
- Being able to view self with a reasonable sense of self-worth
- Being able to cope with problem-solving and decision-making without being driven by self-reference

The problem with any definition is that it is always incomplete. You may read this as a checklist, but perhaps a further definition of emotional maturity should read: 'being able to read definitions of emotional maturity without feeling completely immature'.

What follows is an exercise in knowing about our feelings. Maturity is strongly serviced by awareness. If you know 'what you feel' you can begin to learn 'why you feel it', and with this new knowledge you will be able to have greater control over your life and leadership.

Think about how you feel when confronted with the following (you may wish to record your responses):

- an authority figure
- an elderly person
- an attractive member of the opposite sex
- a poor person
- a police officer
- a child
- a school headteacher
- a person from a foreign country
- a bank manager

- an employer
- a senior denominational figure.

You may want to add to this list if you are aware that there are 'people types' who cause you an emotional shift when you meet them.

Reflection

Reflect on the collection of feelings you have listed and think about the causes that may exist for those feelings. You may be helped by looking back at the lifeline diagram to see if you can make connections between your life and your feelings.

You could repeat this exercise by looking at scenarios that may have feelings attached to them. Here are a few examples:

- When I am disagreed with in a leaders' meeting
- When I am among a crowd of other Christian leaders
- When someone accuses me
- When someone criticises me
- When people say that they love me
- When people don't return my calls
- When my name is left off the list
- When I am thanked for something I have done

Again reflect on your list of feelings, looking for linked causes. The links themselves, once made, provide us with added self-awareness and may help us to bring to mind our inner track when next in those circumstances, and empower us to greater maturity as we take steps in life and work.

Remember, if you have difficulty with this, and if your emotional stability is disturbed to the point where you feel raw and vulnerable, you may want to seek the help of a counsellor who can support your growth in all of this.

Emotional maturity and spiritual values

The Western world has been described as a 'rat race' by many because of its competitive nature. It certainly seems to value a life driven by the need to succeed, with success referenced by personal wealth. The more we acquire, the more successful we are seen to be. This points to a lifestyle that encourages self-worth through financial growth and is a highly destructive dynamic. Christian spirituality opposes wealth as the source of self-worth and in its place offers a message of God's love: 'The LORD appeared to us in the past, saying: "I have loved you with an everlasting love; I have drawn you with loving-kindness"' (Jer. 31:3). As Christians, we may draw inner strength and self-worth from the fact that we are loved by God, *as we are*; not for what we do or how well we perform in a given set of circumstances, or for how much money we may have. This is part of the freeing, peace-giving nature of the Christian walk. Where this belief system forms part of the inner terms of reference, greater emotional maturity and personal peace are experienced. We experience difficulty when this belief is held not so much in our hearts as our heads; when we give academic assent to this, but it is not a core belief from which we draw strength.

There exists for many Christians a gap between belief and life, a kind of disintegrated faith that compartmentalises spirituality. Many Christian leaders will admit to preaching a message of peace without really knowing this peace in their inner being. This would be the difference between faith as a theory and faith as a lifestyle. Emotional maturity is greatly enhanced for those whose inner or core beliefs are at one with their spirituality, where God's love and approval of people enable them to live life with a greater level of peace, without the need to prove themselves worthy in a highly competitive society.

Preferences and prejudices

If our decision-making processes are able to be affected by our emotional track, then so can our views be. If you have been closely following the discussion so far and have been engaging with some of the exercises, then you may be able to see that some of your choices and beliefs have been influenced by your comfort zones. I have found that many leaders who have been growing in their self-awareness have gone back over their belief system about God, church and life itself and have discovered that some of their beliefs and preferences have been coloured by their own lack of self-worth. Self-awareness enhances the sincerity of our beliefs and increases our communicative integrity as we seek to lead in God's Church.

Personality and gifting

Case study

Eric James, a Pentecostal minister from Scotland, practised hard at being the 'charismatic leader' of his congregation. He had understood the role of minister as one undertaken by an extrovert personality constantly seen and heard. He found himself being deliberately loud at church functions and spending much of his time circulating among the people. He hardly ever sat with his own family at fellowship meals and found that he was always 'in role' when with other people from the church. He came to me to talk about his exhaustion in his role. The energy it took for Eric to carry out his ministry was such that he was constantly tired and didn't look forward to church functions. He was not out of balance with work and leisure, but was simply ill at ease with his role and was now wondering whether he was, in his own words, 'not cut out to be a minister'.

A few simple questions began to shed light on the cause of the tiredness. Eric was attempting to perform as a different personality – he was not living true to himself. He had confused his understanding of ministry role with a certain 'personality type', and had assumed that all ministers must be this way. He had mostly observed those whom he believed to be successful Christian leaders as extrovert personalities and tried to be one. His own preference was not to be the centre of attention and not to be the 'life and soul' of every gathering. He was in reality a more introverted personality whose ministry gifts were enhanced by his ability for reflection and contemplation and his love of silence. He could more easily meet with God in the quiet place rather than the crowd. This did not preclude him from ministry, but required him to think through the difference between personality and ministry role.

In truth, people vary in many ways: they think, feel, desire and act differently. When confronted with the same situation, one person will laugh, while another will cry, and a third will grow angry. We all read circumstances differently and deal with people in different ways. Clearly human beings fit into different personality types.

For example, the world-famous Myers–Briggs Type Indicator (MBTI) identifies four main streams of personality type that may come together to produce sixteen different subtypes of people. Eric and others make the mistake of judging some types to be better than others. One important fact must be noted: no one personality type is better or worse than any other. Each is evidenced in the general population and occurs at different frequencies, and some are more common than others. Each psychological type has its own learning style.

With regard to growing self-awareness, knowing your personality type with its typical attributes can be helpful in a number of ways:

- I can discover my learning style and improve my ability to learn
- I can see more clearly where I may fit into a leadership team
- I can accept a leadership role more suited to my personality

Most human beings are happier and work better in areas and in ways of interest to them and that match their personality type. I call this simply 'putting round pegs in round holes'. There is a measure of fear and suspicion in some Christian circles over this level of self-understanding but I believe that it is simply acknowledging how God has made us and being good stewards of who we are in Him. Personality-type indicators are not designed to be the last word or indeed to pretend to know everything about us and so to relegate us to some personality 'pigeon hole', but instead should be freeing indicators in order to facilitate life choices. The MBTI is world-renowned and well-documented. I recommend that all Christian leaders take a test of this nature as part of their journey of self-awareness. A large number of the issues that crop up between Christian leaders and their churches, leadership teams or church members are caused by the clash of personalities. Increased personality awareness will help to solve many of these issues.

The following exercise can be undertaken only by those who have taken a personality-type test. These are widely available and can also be accessed via the Internet:

- What personality type am I?
- What impact does my type have on my role?
- What are the strengths and weaknesses of my type in my role?

A similar discussion can be had with regard to 'gifting'. There exists for Christians a wide view of the nature of spiritual gifts and their source.

Generally the facts that gifts are available and that all Christians will have them are acceptable to most. The issue rarely discussed is the question of how we acknowledge these gifts and release them. There also exists an under-developed view of how such gifts relate to leadership roles.

Great tension exists for Christian leaders who live with the congregational expectation of certain gifts from their role without actually possessing those gifts. Some Christian leaders are called to be the minister of a church, which for many implies 'preaching', without being gifted in public speaking. Some are engaged as pastors when their main gifting is that of preaching or evangelism. Occupational stress is experienced here, when what is required is a more highly developed view of gifting in its relationship to role. In my experience many ministers struggle with their roles because they are not gifted for the whole package that has evolved through the history of the Church. A pastor may not be a preacher, or an evangelist may make a poor pastor! Few Christian leaders are omnigifted.

A number of 'gift indicators', such as the Modified Houtts Questionnaire, form a similar style to the 'question-and-answer' motif of personality-testing. These gift indicators help individuals recognise areas in which they are likely to be gifted. These tests are not necessarily the 'voice of God', and are not intended to block or discourage individuals so much as to point through what may be an 'awareness fog' to what gifts they may be able to exercise.

The following is an exercise requiring a fair amount of courage. Do it only if you feel comfortable doing so.

- What are my three main areas of gifting as far as I understand them today?
- What are my three secondary areas of gifting as I understand them today?
- Am I working as a Christian leader in harmony with my gifting?

Perhaps one of the greatest difficulties in encouraging the unbeliever to become a follower of Christ is the matter of congruence between the Christian and the preached message. When a minister preaches a message of incredible peace it can become obvious to the onlooker that the preacher does not know the peace of which he or she speaks.

Working with increased self-awareness can help Christian leaders to become more integrated people. They are able to live out what they believe and to be at greater peace within themselves. They are able to tap into the love God has for them, giving them a greater sense of well-being and self-esteem. Surely part of the Christian message must be that all people are created equal and that the Father loves each one?

This book is based on the need for increased self-awareness and the foregoing has been but an introduction to a vast theme.

2. Journal Writing in the Ministry

Using a journal is an age-old practice undertaken by people from many walks of life and religious persuasions. This chapter will help you to see how such a practice may help you in both your journey of self-awareness and your spiritual journey.

What is a journal?

Keeping a journal is a particularly useful tool in the quest for self-awareness. It enables us to stay in touch with what is going on in our lives and allows us to express what we feel, when we feel it. What follows is an overview of different understandings of the use of a journal and then some practical suggestions as to how we may benefit from this process. One of my favourite writings is *The Journal of John Wesley*. I can spend hours imagining the situations he found himself in and how he felt about them. Wesley's journalling model is strong and influential, but today's Christian leaders may be unable to see the purpose and benefits of journalling or be unable to spare the time they think is required. The pace of life for the modern leader is much more hurried, but there are many benefits to writing a journal and various ways of achieving it.

The journal as a record

For some, like Wesley, a journal is a record of daily events ('journal' literally means 'daily'). This may suit those personalities who like both the routine of daily recording and keeping an ongoing flow of life events as they happen, providing the writer with a full record of life.

For others a journal is a weekly exercise; an opportunity to reflect on the events of the week, a little like the weekly news round-up. This is another helpful model and is more suited to the personality who feels hampered by daily recording.

For yet others a journal is added to when the time seems right or when they have something to say. This is the approach of those who find journal writing a chore (the enemy of journalling) if they have to stick to a routine. These people use the journal only when they feel it would be helpful to do so.

The diary approach to journalling is limited to the realm of recording events and perhaps the establishment of good time-management principles. To make the greatest use of the art of journalling it is necessary to take the process into a different realm.

The journal as a personal growth/self-awareness tool

This use of the journal requires the individual to opt for a more regular and disciplined approach to the process. It involves the development of a life habit that the individual can grow to love. It is not so much the use of a journal to *record* the inner journey as a tool to *aid* the inner journey. It enables the writer to be in touch and stay in touch.

If you were going to adopt this helpful practice, then you would need to make a covenant with yourself to put space into each day or number of days (too infrequent an interval detracts from the overall benefits) to work with your journal. It sounds a little like developing the practice of personal devotions, and in fact your journalling can form part of your devotional life, as will be explained later.

Journalling works best if it is something you enjoy doing. People are often more motivated if they look forward to something. It may sound strange but you can grow to look forward to the time in each day that you give over to this activity.

Your choice of environment is important to your journal writing (though not always something that you can shape). Where possible, select a comfortable and peaceful place to do your journalling. Also select a medium for your journal that is pleasing to you. When I let my imagination work, I think of a burgundy leather-bound book with a Victorian feel to it. I imagine a shelf full of these books filed in chronological order. I also imagine a Victorian study with a leather chair in matching burgundy, and brass oil lamps – but I don't have any of those things! It's a pleasant dream, but in reality I prefer to use my computer for journalling and there are programs available that can be enormously helpful. I write my sermons at the computer and all my writing is done there. It is a textual home for me and I am comfortable with this medium. The important thing is to find out what works for you.

The atmosphere in which you write your journal, in a way similar to that of the environment, has an effect on this process. What goes on around you affects the possibility of positive reflection. You will do better if you can achieve stillness and silence, and it is preferable if you are alone. Much of this comes with practice. Silence is not something that simply omits sound, but something that moves beyond the loudness of our own thoughts to a deeper place of reflection.

Your personal attitude can also affect this process. Listening to yourself as you begin your journalling time is important. Perhaps writing down everything you feel as you begin each session is helpful.

For example, your session may begin with something like this: 'I feel tired and hurried after a busy day. I have been a little hurt by some criticism about my pastoral care, and it has made me feel quite angry. I don't feel quiet inside, or still, and I have to force myself to write these things down. Instead I want to punch the wall.' Later in the session it may turn to this: 'I was hurt because I know that my pastoral care as a minister is the hardest work for me. I am not naturally gifted in this area. I am angry because someone pressed one of my buttons by telling me a truth that I don't particularly like The truth is that I am not good at it and the criticism was fair.' This could further lead to: 'I must talk with the leadership team about my involvement with pastoral visiting. I am not sure that I am the best choice for this necessary task.'

Without the reflection that journalling provides, the fictitious minister might have gone on being hurt and angry and have passed this hurt on to whoever happened to come within range. Acknowledging what you feel and then reflecting on it is a very worthwhile process.

When studying, I have learned that writing things down helps me to retain information that I need to keep. So I write notes when I revise for exams, and this helps me to keep in touch with the subject matter. We all differ here to some degree, but it is generally accepted that recording detail in writing helps with information retention. Part of the beauty of the journal is that you also have it as a record of feelings, and that you can look back and learn from it. This helps to make your daily experiences tools for the present and the future.

For example: 'On reading my journal over the last few months I am aware that I feel particularly peaceful when I am fishing. My stress levels have been very high these last three weeks. I think I can control this by taking a fishing trip.' OK, so we don't all like fishing, but knowing what patterns of tension and peace are being set up in your life in the past through journalling can inform you about dealing with events in the present. It's a little like retaining useful information that belongs to you that hitherto you would have discarded.

It is helpful in this process if your journal records the range of dates that you are covering with each new entry, including the date (month, day and year), day of the week and the time. If you are in a special place, you could note that as well, with a description of your surroundings, and perhaps a brief review of the events leading to your being at that place. This will further enhance the accuracy and usefulness of your reflections.

For example: 'I can see from past entries that when I am staying at Tom and Sarah's, I don't feel very rested. I experience a degree of hostility from Tom, who longed to be a leader in our church before he moved away, and the leadership team didn't think that he was ready for that role at the time.'

It can also be helpful to record with each entry what you consider your mood to be. This, over a period of time, can put you in touch with mood swings and their causes. You can learn to change negative mood swings positively if you can discover what causes them.

Recording your current health level as you go also provides you with important information. Periods of prolonged stress can lead to a weakened ability to fight off colds and flu. If you have been experiencing periods of minor ill health, your journal may have tracked the reasons for this and may provide you with some answers. You can learn from the journalling process what may help to keep you in optimum health. There can be a distinct relationship between your health and your life activity.

Similarly, recording stress levels may give you positive indicators as to which activities cause you to experience the most stress. If you record how stressed you are feeling, you may then learn how to avoid or manage these dynamics. The *Life Journal* (a computerised journal by the Chronicles Software Company, www.lifejournal.com) provides you with a numerical value to help you chart your stress, mood, energy and health, and then allows you to view them on an interactive graph. This is an enormously helpful process. Recording how well or how badly you slept the night before is helpful. Sleep is a necessary restorative process and interrupted patterns increase the stress and strain of your life. A journal can keep you in touch with what causes you to sleep well or badly, and can facilitate healthier sleep patterns through the learning process.

A debate about the importance and place of dreams continues in the halls of psychology and theology, but what we do know is that our subconscious produces stories in the form of dreams. Dreams appear to be a kind of data processing of information stored in our subconscious dealing with both fact and fantasy. These dreams are bizarre at times, but recording in your journal what you remember can be quite illuminating when viewed alongside the other recorded data. Whatever your preferred view of dreams, writing them down gives you data to reflect upon what is created by your own mind.

I remember from my school days being told that talking to yourself is a sign of madness. (Not that I ever did, you understand!) However, I have discovered, since those days, that most of us talk to ourselves mentally several times a day. We all engage in self-dialogue, and you may find it helpful to record in your journal what you are saying (in your mind) to yourself.

Devotional life and journalling

Similarly, writing to God is a helpful journalling process. It can help you get in touch with what you want to say. It gets the 'inside' out! Using the journal as part of your devotional life can help you to hold a dialogue with God on the written page. As I look back to my journal of some ten years ago I realise that I can see my joys and suffering and see the hand of God in my life both then and now. I am able to see how God has worked in my life over those ten years. Like the psalmist, I can look back and gain strength to move forward from here. I can tell God how I am feeling and release to Him the stresses and strains, highs and lows of my life. I can also record my prayer requests, then look back when I have His answers and be encouraged.

You can also use the journal to record your spiritual experiences: those moments when you feel that God has been particularly close or life feels like a spiritual desert. The journal becomes a spiritual record for you. When viewed against mood swings and stress levels you will be able to see the cause of some of your spiritual peaks and troughs and grow in your understanding of your spirituality.

I would certainly encourage you in the use of a journal in your journey of self-awareness. Get a book or a computer program that you are comfortable with and begin. Don't worry if your first attempts seem like short entries. This is a growing process that often starts with just a few lines.

On page 38 is an example of how you might lay out your journal pages. This is simply an example. It is most important that you use the medium that suits you best. For me, it is a computerised journal that sets up my daily page automatically. I have used several different types including one that works on my hand-held device. I am able to password-protect my entry and so keep my journal in a safe place.

Protecting the privacy of your journal is important, whatever type of journal you may prefer, because the more confidential a tool it becomes the more you will trust it as a safe place to record your most private thoughts. This can help you to add depth to your journalling.

Ronald Klug, in his book *How to Keep a Spiritual Journal*, lists ten good reasons for keeping a journal:

- Growth in self-understanding
- An aid to the devotional life
- Guidance and decision-making
- Making sense and order of life
- Releasing emotions and gaining perspective
- Greater awareness of daily life
- Self-expression and creativity
- Clarifying beliefs
- Setting goals and managing time
- Working through problems

Happy journalling!

Date and time	Title for entry	Place	Mood, stress, health, etc

Page no.

3. The Call to Ministry

Calling, much like guidance, seems to be an elusive business. Most of us would wish that the writing was on the wall, but it isn't. We rely on a non-exact science, such as interpreting a Scripture passage, receiving the encouragement of others, hearing the inner voice and, for some, receiving a prophetic word.

During my ministry training I asked one of the other students how he had experienced his sense of calling and to what he was called. I think I was struggling with doubt about my own sense of call. I hadn't seen any flashing lights or heard any voices and was unsure what exactly God was asking me to do. I had gone through all the interviews and other tests and had passed 'fit for training', but internally I was in turmoil. On reflection, inner doubt about how to serve God may be a healthy trait that keeps us current and dependent on God for what we offer in His service. But at the time it felt as though I was lacking in faith. A fellow student said, 'I am going to be an international evangelist.' His confident understanding of his calling stunned me! I could not be nearly as clear and concise about what I had experienced, but I did feel as if God was quietly telling me that I was to train for the ministry. On sharing this with others they agreed with my conviction.

At the end of four years in theological college I was the proud owner of a degree in theology and a diploma in pastoral studies, and was standing in a line, on a beautiful lawn in the college grounds, waiting to go onto a stage in a crowded marquee to tell the gathered crowd about my call to ministry. Other students were leafing through scriptures to find the passage God had used to 'call' them into the ministry. I was very nervous. I hadn't got a passage or an event to back up my call to the ministry! What if I was an imposter, not called at all?

Looking back, I am aware that my doubts and fears were tied up in the whole range of questions that need to be considered regarding an understanding of a 'calling'.

- Where does our understanding of calling come from?
- How do we interpret it?
- What are we called to?

- Is everybody called?
- Is there a particular calling to ministry?
- Are there unique stressors connected to calling?

This chapter will help you to consider the subject of calling and enable you to reflect on your own experience and understanding.

Where does our understanding of calling come from?

Historical

In part our current understanding will be influenced by our own spiritual history. You and I will have gained insights from those significant spiritual milestones, such as conversion, along the way. If you had a conversion experience and a Christian minister was either a significant part of the experience or an early influence after the event, then your view of ministry will be coloured by this. If you were brought up in the Church, then that experience could also be seen to be an influence on your current understanding. What you have seen and heard through your life will undoubtedly affect your understanding. The past frequently visits the present.

Denominational

Your early experience of church and ministry will also influence your outlook, together with your denominational preference. It is true that many ministers or leaders work in independent settings, but your understanding is likely to have been affected by the local church that has been most influential in your life. For instance, I may be a Baptist with one view of the ministry that differs from another view held by people from another Baptist church. My denomination and its local expression may be linked but separate sources of my understanding. Where you prefer a denomination in your chosen spiritual journey, you may be greatly influenced in your understanding of the ministry and of calling by this stance. Where a local expression of the denomination views ministry slightly differently from the denominational stance, the local expression may be the dominant influence.

Reflection

How far do you think these things have affected your understanding of the ministry and calling? Are you able to take a pace backwards and have a clearer overview?

Theological

Your understanding of the ministry may be influenced by your theological grasp. Your own reading of Scripture may directly influence you or, more typically, you may be influenced by an interpretation of Scripture passed to you by significant others. These significant others could be a minister, a lecturer, a parent, a friend, an author, etc. This is not to say that we are incapable of free thought, but that there is a lot less of it around than we may imagine.

I would love to be able to say that all my thoughts and beliefs are my own, but it would be a proud and untrue statement. Many of the positions I have held through the years, I now realise, were given to me by well-meaning and equally convinced others. Few of my beliefs originated with me. This is true for all human beings, but maturity for me is in part the arrival at my own belief system rather than one that is second-hand. Many others may espouse the beliefs I end up with, but I hold them now as my own and am stronger for it. The journey of self-awareness includes taking a good look at what you believe.

It was a great shock to me the day when, as a parent, I became 'my mother'. I caught myself passing on to my son the exact words and point of view about some of his adolescent behaviour that my mother had given to me. I hadn't processed the view at all; I simply trusted my mother's judgment and passed it on. My son, in his adoption of another adolescent motif, questioned my judgment with such sound logic that I was caught adrift with my thinking. I realised that I did not agree with my mother's views on this issue, once I had thought about it. A great victory for my son, and a greater lesson for me!

Reflection

- What do I believe about my calling to the ministry?
- Where do I get my beliefs?
- Who has influenced my thinking about this?
- Do I own my own belief here?

Interpreting a calling

So far, I have pointed to the various influences on our understanding, and these will also play a part in how we interpret our calling. Our view of our calling will be inextricably linked with how we understand the role or office to which we are being called.

Through the centuries a view has grown up that has differentiated between the call of a Christian to any work, and the call of a Christian to the professional pastor/preacher/administrator role that has become traditional for the ordained clergy of most denominations. This has happened to the extent that 'the ministry' is seen almost as an elite, professional Christian role. The strengths of this include the realisation that the role of Christian leader requires serious application, study and commitment. The weaknesses include the establishment of a ready-made identity that can be seen to be attractive to those seeking a short route to what they believe would help them to feel significant.

The need for identity is powerful in the Western world and much of life is given over to its pursuit. A form of tribalism, evidenced by the mighty fashion industry, can be seen to exist, where dressing right, eating right and looking right are powerful messages dominating the media. Society can be divided up into people groups or tribes with their own unwritten codes of conduct. The Church can be seen to be one of these tribes, one that provides identity or social distinctives for its members and in particular for its leaders. In my ministry experience a number of people who have expressed the desire to enter 'the ministry' have frequently alarmed me. It is not the desire itself that has been alarming but the conversations that have gone with it. Many have seen the 'ordained ministry' as the answer to their feelings of inadequacy. The Church embraces a labelling dynamic that enables it to describe function and delineate purpose as a means of managing its existence. Different church types use differing labels: vicar, pastor, minister, deacon, elder, overseer, house group leader, cell group leader, evangelist, counsellor, teacher, preacher, to name but a few. It is possible to gain an immediate sense of identity related to a role by gaining the rank that one of these labels may suggest.

Others have looked to the ministry label because they have considered that God may be a better boss to work for than their current manager. Yet others feel that they don't perform well in the 'secular world' and that life would be easier to cope with if they gave their energies to the 'spiritual world'. This dangerous form of dualism sees the role of ministers as other-worldly, a kind of mystical spiritual experience that keeps them from the ordinary business of life. In its worst case, the ministry can be perceived as a spiritual safe haven to which one may flee if life is difficult to face. The removal of the ministry from ordinary life enhances the mysticism surrounding the role and adds to the view that the ministry is somehow a higher function for God than anything else.

These thoughts raise the uncomfortable question of how far we are able to interpret as a calling to the ministry the desire for significance and identity. Is it possible that many of us offer ourselves for ministry training driven by this sense of inner need? This is not to suggest that many have an illegitimate calling so much as to recognise that God may use various means to reach out to us.

Reflection

Has this discussion prompted any recognisable feelings within you? Reflect on these thoughts and feelings.

The need for identity can seriously shape the experience of our ministry. A sense of threat can be perceived if other members of our church want to exercise gifting similar or superior to our own. In a later chapter of this book the subject of 'ministry burnout' will be addressed. This condition can be brought about in part by 'drivenness' in ministry, related to the fear of allowing anyone to help you since that help may detract from your sense of identity. Typically a minister will do all of the preaching if they interpret preaching as a primary function of the role. For some, allowing anyone else to preach detracts from their role and, in truth, creates a tension in them, from the fear that the preacher may make a better job of it than they do.

Reflection

How far is your identity linked with your ministry role?

The ministry

Having discussed briefly some of the psychosocial aspects surrounding 'calling' and 'identity', the subject would be incomplete without further discussion as to what is meant by 'the ministry'. As previously mentioned, throughout church history a view has grown up that has differentiated between the call of a Christian to any work, and the call of a Christian to the professional pastor/preacher/administrator role that has become traditional for the ordained clergy of most denominations. The very nature of the Church as the *ekklésia* includes the concept of the whole Church comprising the community of the 'called-out ones'. There exists for all Christians everywhere a sense in which they are all called to be followers of Christ and to live according to His teaching.

The teaching of the New Testament outlines a lifestyle that differs significantly from that whose driving force for life is self-interest (see for example the Sermon on the Mount). Biblical books such as 1 Corinthians and Ephesians espouse a doctrine of giftedness that points to what is often called 'body ministry' – concepts that were significantly highlighted in the 1970s and 1980s by books like *The Body* by Chuck Swindoll. This view of Church suggests that all Christians are called: first by God to Himself and then to acts of body ministry according to their gifting.

In the New Testament, the language of calling primarily refers to the call of God to become a Christian (Rom. 1:6–7; 8:28–30; 1 Cor. 1:9; Gal. 1:6). Paul also uses it in connection with his commissioning to be an apostle of Christ (Rom. 1:1; 1 Cor. 1:1). But we need to be careful about generalising from such texts because of the direct way in which God chose the apostles for a specific task.

At one level, Paul urges people to remain in the state or condition in which they were called to be Christians and to honour God by transformed attitudes and behaviour in that context (1 Cor. 7:17–24). Everyday life and work is the sphere in which to explore what it means to be Christian and to serve God. In the sense that God has enabled someone to become a Christian teacher, a mother, an advertising agent or a doctor, we could say that this is a 'calling', though Scripture does not talk this way.

At another level, it is clear that evangelism and strengthening the churches was a priority for Paul. Sometimes he encouraged others to leave their previous commitments and join him in this work in a full-time way (Acts 12:25; 15:40; 16:1–3). He also encouraged those with various ministries to engage in equipping the saints for the work of the ministry of the Church (Eph. 4:11–12).

People today may be similarly drawn by the teaching of Scripture, the need for gospel ministry and a sense of God's gifting, to offer themselves for full-time ministry. Are they then called by God? It may be a legitimate way of describing God's leading and provision for them once their suitability for a particular ministry has been tried and tested. But there is a danger in using the term with the same confidence Paul did. A person may not be called to the Christian ministry as traditionally understood, even though they have become convinced that it is God's will.

Called to what?

As a result of the above, some people sense a call of God on their lives and immediately interpret it as a call to the professional Christian ministry, when in fact they are being encouraged by God to the ministry of whatever they do best: to live for God in their immediate surroundings and 'minister' the gospel to others through their lifestyle. A person may not be called to the professional Christian ministry but can become convinced of it. Discussing their sense of call with others may only serve to encourage them further down the wrong path since many view 'calling' as belonging to the Christian ministry or the mission field alone. This is due, in part, to the lack of communication about the many and various callings God may place on our lives.

The first question to answer when sensing a call is, what am I called to? It is important at this stage that a person discuss this sense of call with someone else whom they trust to be objective and with whom they may talk freely about gifting and personality, in order to help ground the call and encourage its best direction. The life changes that take place for the Christian minister are such that it is far better to discover that you are not called to this area of service while you are not serving in the role.

Reflection

What do you consider you were called by God to do?

Motivation behind calling

Probably most people begin to consider their calling either from within (a sense of something that God may be saying) or from without (others suggest that God may be calling them to what they understand to be 'the ministry' as opposed to 'a ministry'). When looking at the subject of calling it is important to recognise that there is nothing straightforward about this. Few people get up in the morning to see their name written in the clouds along with a description of a proposed area of ministry. Many will simply have an inner sense of something. They may read a scripture and feel personally spoken to, or someone else may have planted the seed by saying something like 'God wants you in the ministry'. They may have attended a meeting where an appeal to come forward to 'offer your life for deeper Christian service' has been given and have responded to it emotionally. There are many reasons why people believe that they are called to ministry. I believe in a God who may use any means to get the attention of His servants.

What follows is a consideration of some of the motivation that surrounds the subject of calling.

Emotionalism

Emotions play an important part in the life of a human being and it is not unrealistic to assume that God may choose to use our emotions as a means of getting us to engage in some particular form of Christian service. However, the engaging of our emotions alone is not sufficient evidence of God's call. Many forms of Christian worship evoke emotional responses into which appeals are frequently made. At best this is well-meaning; at worst it can be a form of coercion to particular activities such as giving or acts of service. Responding to a particularly powerful appeal to serve because of our own heightened emotions could be evidence of God, but it may simply be an emotional response at that moment, which cannot sustain a lifetime of ministry.

Guilt

Some people have a sense of guilt when they think about God – possibly as the result of their upbringing or their early experiences of Christian teaching where God has been understood to be a strict, wrathful being. Often deep-rooted, these feelings can lead to a low sense of self-worth and a subservient attitude to life in general. Guilty feelings, earned or imagined, may result in a desire to please God through some sacrificial act such as entering the ministry.

Case study

Gina and Greg were both missionaries working abroad for a well-known missionary organisation. They had both come from difficult backgrounds as children where their parents had been involved with drugs and had shown abusive behaviour. Gina and Greg had both entered into this lifestyle and had developed serious drug and behavioural problems. By the grace of God they had come to know Him and had found in their relationship with Him the strength to give up their habits.

After a few years Gina and Greg went to Bible school and this is where they met and eventually married. They were no longer living their lives in the drug scene and had amended their antisocial behaviour patterns, but were left quite emotionally scarred by their former lives. Gina and Greg were so thankful to God for saving them from their former lives that they wanted to serve Him for ever, and interpreted this as a call to overseas mission (seen as a hard life but a valid response to God's love). They were accepted for service and soon found themselves in a foreign land with little support, 'serving the Lord in mission'.

Before much time had passed (a matter of a few months), Gina and Greg began to struggle with the work. They felt lonely and overwhelmed in a foreign culture and gradually began to feel like failures. This reached a peak and they came to see me for counselling. As we discussed their situation it became apparent that they were not so much answering a call to the mission field as pacifying a God before whom they felt guilty about their family background and former lives. They felt so badly about their past that they wanted to make up for it by 'hard labour', as they saw it. They felt they could pay God back for His goodness towards them. They felt so unworthy of His love that it seemed as though they should spend their lives paying.

This, in a sense, was another form of abusive behaviour they were living out. It was as if God wanted to abuse them with a hard life before they could receive any good gift of His. Gina and Greg needed to return from the mission field and take time out in counselling before they could begin to know if they were in the right place. It could be that God's call to them would be to some other form of service.

Guilt-based service is particularly draining of human energy and is usually unrewarding. Like a bottomless pit that can never be filled, no amount of service seems to be a large enough payment for our sin. Guilty people go on feeling guilty until they have embraced the grace of God in forgiveness and until that same forgiveness has become a core belief and part of the bedrock of life.

The quest for power

Can it be true that someone would offer themselves for the ministry with such a quest? I think so. Not because the ministry represents a significant influence in terms of the big wide world but because some people have observed the professional Christian minister and have decided that they are in a desirable position in terms of power and influence in the Church. Consciously or unconsciously, they desire to be in this position of 'favour'. Some feel that those in the Christian ministry have been picked by God as unique human beings, a kind of 'super-Christian elite', and they long to be numbered among this special band of people. This view and subsequent hope may often stem from a person's low self-esteem. The Christian ministry can be seen as a ladder to instant significance but, in truth, this ministry is special only in the sense that any ministry role is special: it is a service role for God, as is banking, or being a shop assistant, police or fire officer, office worker, dentist, teacher, postal delivery worker, and so on.

The quest for personal power or significance is not a valid response to the call to serve God. It is not indicative of a call to Christian ministry so much as a window on a person's insecurity.

Disappointment

I have spoken to many people who had hoped that God was calling them to the Christian ministry. Some had become so upset about the fact that the doors seemed to close for them that they had become angry and bitter. One young man had so set his hopes on this that he left the Church. He had complained when, once again, he had not been chosen to be a house group leader and had not been allowed to preach in the services. He believed that the life of the Christian was a journey of maturity that led by promotion to places of more and more influence, until one reached the dizzy heights of 'minister'. He yearned for personal significance, because he had been unable to see that the highest place to which any human being can aspire is to be a child of God.

Many people have devalued this wonderful truth. Once we have this, as a free gift through Christ, then there is no ladder up, just acts and roles of service. We live in a world where rank, status and position are rewarded by financial gain. 'Up' in the world seems so desirable and we make so many comparisons with others as we look for our worth. Worth in the kingdom of God, where we are loved and valued by Him, is immediate and instant. We cannot earn worth by adopting a worldly system of advancement.

Those of us who are disappointed and feel rejected or barred from the Christian ministry must remember that we all have gifts and abilities that can be used for God that are of equal value and are part of Christian ministry.

There clearly exists a genuine 'call' to serve God, and for some that will be a call to Christian leadership or to pastoral service that in today's Church is often given recognition through ordination and/or designation as priest, vicar, pastor, minister, etc. This chapter has sought to help you consider the nature of your own sense of call, not so much to bring you a sense of doubt about what you do, but to help you to be increasingly aware of yourself and your beliefs and experiences. The discovery of feelings, motives and influences is not to suggest that you are wrongly placed in leadership so much as to enable you to have a mature and informed overview of the various nuances surrounding the subject of calling.

Stress and calling

A later section of the book will look at this in greater depth. However, it is important to note here that the stress experienced in your ministry may be directly linked to the understanding of your ministry call. If you are simultaneously preacher, teacher, administrator, pastor, evangelist and counsellor, then you are likely to be suffering under a huge and unnatural measure of stress from a highly complex and overburdened view of ministry. Such a man or woman would truly be superhuman.

Ministry baggage

This book recognises that God calls 'people' to Christian ministry, to work in His Church, in many denominations and church types. The one thing that all who enter this form of service have in common is that they are human: they all have a past and a developmental history.

As you continue through this book, remember that you will bring your own 'baggage' to your Christian service. This baggage is the collection of psychological, emotional and spiritual dynamics that have affected your life. Some characteristics will be positive and health-giving, and others will be negative and destructive. Part of your journey of discovery and growth will be to get in touch with your 'baggage' and effectively repack the bag. Let this book and its various suggested exercises assist you in your personal journey. Desire to be honest with yourself and with God, to hone and sharpen your gifting in order to be increasingly effective as you serve Him.

Reflection

Reflect on this chapter. Record what has made you feel both positive and negative, and what information about you and your ministry it has brought to the surface.

4. Expectation and the Ministry

Each year many hundreds of holidaymakers head off for their two weeks in the sun, only to find that the photos in the glossy travel agent brochure bear little relation to their final destination. The swimming pool is merely a bath. The restaurant, complete with apple-mouthed, hog-head dishes, turns out to be 'El Sandwicho Baro', bearing nothing more than plates of limp cheese salads. Bedrooms with a view are just that, offering splendid views over the car park to the hotel next door. What a let down! Television companies have made whole series about it all.

Christian ministry can be just like this. OK, maybe not the limp cheese salads, but certainly tainted with unrealistic expectations, with inner pictures of how it will be and what to expect. In Chapter 3, I made the following statement: 'If you are simultaneously preacher, teacher, administrator, pastor, evangelist and counsellor, then you are likely to be suffering under a huge and unnatural measure of stress from a highly complex and overburdened view of ministry. Such a man or woman would truly be superhuman.' Your own understanding of the ministry, how you see it unfolding and working out, will largely govern what expectations you may have for your role. If you have unrealistic expectations of yourself and others, then you are more likely to be disappointed.

Expectations are an important issue in the life of the Christian leader. Some expect little and are therefore quite surprised by their experiences, but by far the majority of leaders expect too much of themselves and feel inadequate. Our research showed that 72 per cent of ministers considered church expectations to be among the top ten sources of stress in the ministry.

Reflection

How far do you feel burdened by the expectations you are aware of?

False expectations are at the centre of many broken relationships, between friends, in marriage and also between a minister and the recipients of that ministry, whatever type of ministry it may be. Expectations need to be uncovered because they are often hidden deep within us. Sometimes they lie undiscovered until we suffer the pain of their non-realisation. Only then do we know that we hurt, without really knowing why.

We need to dig deep within, to examine and understand our expectations. While this cannot be achieved totally, I suggest that those involved in some form of ministry to others need to take a good look at their own expectations and the reasons why these exist.

In the last chapter we looked at the nature of calling and discovered a number of potential problems with our view of ministry. What you believe your calling to be may determine what role you play. The ministering role is so vast that few people in ministry will understand it in exactly the same way as others do. You will bring a personal perception to your work and this perception will carry with it a wide range of expectations. This is only natural.

Some of our expectations are quite obvious but others are not as clear. Expectations could have come to you from anywhere, for example:

- The Bible
- Training school
- Denominational stance
- Personal beliefs
- Family
- Personal ambition

In this chapter I will begin to explore and unpack some of these expectations with a view to grounding them in reality and thus avoiding some of the great problems that can arise. This section will require you to be honest with yourself. It may cause some of you discomfort as you recognise just what you are or have been expecting.

As leaders begin work in the Church there is a matrix of expectations present. They are expecting things of God, themselves and of spouse and family. They will also be the recipient of expectations, both real and imagined, from the Church.

What are you expecting from yourself in this ministry?

Case study

The Revd Raymond Grant began his ministry believing that he had received a call from God and that nothing would or could go wrong. He would sacrifice his life for the sake of the gospel and he expected his family to fall in behind.

- He would preach twice on Sundays as well as lead the services.
- He would hold a prayer meeting on Sunday afternoons.
- An after-fellowship for the young people would follow the evening service.
- He would hold a weekly Bible study.
- He would hold the midweek prayer meeting on another evening.
- He would spend each morning of the rest of the week studying the Bible and preparing his sermons and studies.
- In the afternoons and remaining evenings he would visit the sick, make 'getting to know you' visits and bring helpful counselling to the needy.

He felt sure this would be a plan that would bring health and growth to his church, indeed a grand plan! For the first six months things seemed to be going well. The church seemed to love him and appreciate his efforts. He had allowed his mail and administrative work to slide during this time because he was, after all, 'getting to know the people'.

Before long he began to experience difficulty with his administration. Some of the church committees were asking him where certain documents were and whether he had planned for the next range of meetings to decide the nature of the children's work for the following year. He began to be deluged with administrative work and one of his counsellees kept returning with more problems. No matter what advice he had given, it hadn't worked and this poor person was becoming desperate. Telephone calls and visits to the house began to increase.

His preparation began to be trimmed down until he found himself stretched and highly stressed. He felt he was spending most of his time running from one thing to another. Some of the other leaders asked if they could help, but Raymond believed that by accepting he would be letting the side down. He pressed on until the church meeting where he was told, angrily, that he had kept the entire ministry to himself and seemed not to trust anyone else. He was told that he seemed to let much of his work slide, and asked what he was doing with his time anyway.

Raymond began to sink deeply into depression. He tried to hide all of this from his long-suffering wife, who by now felt like a stranger to him. She felt he had been ignoring her and told him so. Isolation began to be a big problem. Raymond didn't know who his friends were and developed a fear of the members of the congregation, suspecting them of talking about him negatively. He did not know where to turn and in the end broke down, left the church and resigned from the ministry a shattered man with a strained marriage.

This story is true and is unfortunately not an isolated incident. Where did Raymond go wrong?

At first glance, it is possible to think that he had a good plan. His approach to ministry was not untypical and he should have been able to achieve his goals. In fact Raymond had unrealistic expectations. Like so many in ministry, he had never thought through what was reasonable and possible for him to expect from himself and others. He had not considered the effects of his 'one-man church growth' concept:

- Perhaps he believed himself to be the one answer to the church's needs?
- Perhaps he held hidden hopes of personal greatness?
- Perhaps he thought he knew better than others?
- Perhaps he believed that, with a shared sense of call, abusing his marriage would not damage such a spiritual relationship?
- Perhaps he had not considered the impact of sudden changes on a church?
- Perhaps he was so much of an idealist that he lacked a sense of reality?

The expectations we place on ourselves and others may come from places within that need to be changed. Too many ministers expect too much. They often feel that to do otherwise is contrary to *faith*. They have mixed up the concepts of 'what we believe' and 'what we expect'. Belief in the 'all-powerful God' can lead to a belief in the 'all-capable minister'. It can lead to a denial of our humanity and the clear needs and limitations of simply being human and not divine. Ministers bring a personal perception to their work, and this perception carries with it a wide range of expectations. Such expectations lead to a vast array of roles that would commonly be considered to be those of the Christian minister. High levels of stress are experienced as ministers attempt to do far too much. Here is a list of typical ministry expectations gained from our research and my counselling practice. You'll recognise the first seven:

1. Preach twice on Sunday as well as lead the services.
2. Lead a prayer meeting on Sunday afternoon.
3. Lead an after-fellowship for the young people, following the evening service.
4. Lead a weekly Bible study.
5. Lead the midweek prayer meeting on another evening.
6. Spend each morning of the rest of the week studying the Bible and preparing sermons and studies.
7. In the afternoons and remaining evenings visit the sick, make 'getting to know you' visits, and bring helpful counselling to the needy.
8. Spend quality time with spouse and children individually.
9. Be available always at the end of the telephone for the fellowship.
10. Make time for advice or counselling sessions when necessary.
11. Lead funeral services with appropriate aftercare.
12. Marry couples with appropriate premarital counselling.
13. Administrate the constant inflow of mail and church-generated paperwork.
14. Be involved with community relations and projects.
15. Attend denominational meetings.
16. Attend local ministers' professional 'fraternals'.
17. Fund-raise.
18. Write newsletters.
19. Spend quality time praying.
20. Stay fresh and encourage the church in its purpose.

At first glance, this seems to be an acceptable list of tasks for a minister to perform. The negative stress arises from the level to which these tasks will fill a working week. Our research revealed that 85 per cent of the respondents took one day off per week, but that 52 per cent felt that lack of time was a major stress factor in their lives. In working with my clients I have learned that many ministers work a three-phase day (morning, afternoon and evening) at least five days per week, and that they work on average from sixty-five to eighty-five hours per week as they seek to fulfil the perceived demands made upon them. This is a high rate of work that leaves little time for personal and family needs. Much of the minister's work is with people, which can be very draining. Long hours spent working in stressful circumstances is costly, both physically and emotionally.

Dr Edward B. Bratcher called his work, in which he dealt with professional hazards in the ministry, *The Walk on Water Syndrome*.[1] The title alone points to the fact that ministers often have unrealistic expectations of themselves and others. So much so, that they may attempt to walk on water (a divine attribute).

However well communication of role and role expectations has been undertaken these too are subject to a human response and interpretation. This human element may be a significant source of destructive stress as individuals interpret the communication by their level of understanding, theological perspective and personality. Dr Archibald Hart writes:

> Distorted ideas about the nature of the ministry may contribute to depression. Frequently, distorted ideas about what the vocation of ministry actually entails give rise to unreasonable expectations and hence depression. One common idea is that the ministry is a 'sacred task' and a 'high calling,' and that it therefore demands a very unique sort of commitment. This idea is essentially true, but it can easily become twisted and set the pastor up for unreasonable expectations.[2]

Calling and the experience of ministry shaped by expectations are linked. The nature and understanding of one's sense of call will influence how one views that ministry unfolding. I suggest that there is a real link between the stress of ministry and the expectations perceived by ministers as they interpret the nature of the 'call to ministry' to which they are responding.

In discussion with a number of clients from a broad church background, it seems that calling can be understood by ministers in different ways. For many it appears to be understood according to the prevailing view that exists within the denomination, and for others it is the prevailing view of the congregation of which they are a member at the time of receiving the call. For some, a call to ministry is clearly defined and understood, but for others it takes on an almost mystical dynamic, because the sense of call is considered as a distinct mission that God has set for the individual. So, for some a call to ministry has a sense of service from within the Christian community, and for others it is an individual response to a personal message from God.

Case study

George is an Anglican curate from east London who sees his call to ministry as a call to function as a 'priest' of God. He says that he sees this as an act of service for God and His Church. He understands his role as that of a priest and for him this means being a *pontifex* or 'bridge' between people and God. He will help people relate to God and the Church through his prayers, preaching and acts of service.

Case study

Carl is a Baptist minister in training at a west of England theological college. He understands his call as to world evangelism and feels that God has called him to become a roving evangelist. He believes, but is alone in this belief, that he will serve as a local pastor for a few years before his journey into world evangelisation begins.

Both of these men began serving a local church as an ordained minister after finishing their periods of training. Their call seems to be very different and yet both serve as local ministers, albeit in different church types. Since their sense of calling is different, and it is reasonable to assume that calling will differ from person to person, their understanding of their role is not only theologically different but their expectations will also differ widely.

George was clear about his role and began to work as a minister with few significant issues relating to his role. He had a clear ministry model that he was working out, which helped to give substantial shape to his work. Carl, on the other hand, soon became frustrated in the local church. He was finding it difficult to move forward into his evangelistic role, which lacked the clarity of a model and offered little direction, because of the many tasks he had embraced as a local church minister. Expectations led to a less stressful start to life in the ministry for George, whereas Carl became frustrated early on because his expectations were unfulfilled.

Much of the work of the minister is highly stressful and draining. This needs to be taken into account when making working plans or laying out the working week. My experience in the counselling process leads me to conclude that many ministers have made the following errors:

- They planned to do too much.
- They did not leave enough room for the marriage relationship or the other family members.
- They focused their church's movement forward totally on their ministry.
- They built unrealistic goals that would inevitably fail. They may indeed have 'built in' failure.
- They did not leave enough flexible space in the schedule for the 'unexpected'.
- They left little space for others to minister.
- They did not consider the impact of sudden changes on a church.
- They did not consider the impact of their own personality and emotional make-up upon their workload.

These issues are often experienced unconsciously, with the resulting stress and its health-damaging dynamics coming as a complete surprise.

Reflection

Reflect on your role and what you believe it to be, and ask yourself if you are working with a set of realistic expectations.

What are you expecting from your church?

Your understanding of the church will cause you to have a set of expectations of the congregation. These can be as unrealistic as those you have of yourself.

Reflection

Perhaps at this stage it would be good to reflect on what you expect from the church you serve.

Relationship
Confusion, stress and pain can be experienced by ministers as a result of their understanding of their relationship with the church. They may even have hidden expectations. A hidden expectation is not carried in the front of a person's mind but may have a significant impact on how the ministry is experienced.

Case study

The Revd Jim Mortlake had only recently come to his church as pastor. He had been to a theological college and was now placed in his first appointment. He had set a reasonable pace of ministry and was coping with it. The people seemed to appreciate him. In the early months of his ministry people would invite him to their homes for dinner on a regular basis. He seemed the focus of much attention. He enjoyed it and even played up to it, adopting something of a 'showman' stance on Sunday mornings.

As the months went by and his first anniversary passed, Jim noticed that the invitations for dinner had virtually stopped. The attention he had been paid was not the same somehow. People didn't seem so excited by his presence and they had stopped laughing with quite the same energy in his regular, lively Sunday morning presentations.

People seemed less in awe of his ideas and plans for the future. They asked more questions now and challenged his thinking. He felt completely out of favour, and considered himself disliked and unwanted as their minister.

Jim became deeply troubled by what was happening and started to ask serious questions of himself and his preaching. The spark and enjoyment of ministry was dimming for him and he found himself growing depressed. He wondered if he had somehow made a dreadful mistake and come to the wrong church.

In counselling it was discovered that Jim was an only child and enjoyed being the centre of attention. He assumed that he would be the focus of all attention and was transferring his earlier childhood experiences to this setting. Also he had come from a church that seemed to love its minister, and he had expected exactly the same experience. He craved the love and affection of everyone and couldn't cope with indifference. He had understood love to mean that he should constantly be at the centre of an exclusive relationship. His view of love had been distorted by his parent–child relationship. Henri Nouwen comments on this view of love when he writes:

> It is important for me to realize how limited, imperfect, and weak my understanding of love has been. Not my theoretical understanding but my understanding as it reveals itself in my emotional responses to concrete situations. My idea of love proves to be exclusive: 'You only love me truly if you love others less'; possessive: 'If you really love me, I want you to pay special attention to me'; and manipulative: 'When you love me, you will do extra things for me.' Well, this idea of love easily leads to vanity: 'You must see something very special in me'; to jealousy: 'Why are you now suddenly so interested in someone else and not in me?' and to anger: 'I am going to let you know that you have let me down and rejected me.'[3]

Jim felt that being constantly in focus was to be loved, and if this was not happening then he was no longer loved. He began to feel rejected when normal attention levels ensued. Further to this, he had understood good leadership to mean being the centre of attention. He had believed that people would naturally follow his lead because he was 'the minister'. He had not understood or expected that the church would go through a 'honeymoon' period with him. (This is a description of the early ministry period in a new church when everything is new and relationships have not been established.) He had not thought that true relationships grow with time or that trust has to be earned and is not given instantly to people simply because they hold a position. He had not made allowances for human nature and the fact that novelty wears off.

Jim had laid enormous expectations at the feet of the church and was troubled when these were not met. He needed the benefit of counselling in order to make sense of his feelings and experiences. He was stressed by circumstances and seemingly incapable of understanding them. Once he had grown through this experience Jim was able to adjust his expectations and have a more positive experience of the ministry.

This case study illustrates that unrealistic expectations, as stressful as they are, may also come from emotional sources deep in the original family situation. Sometimes there can be a mismatch between the earlier experiences of family and the current experience of church life.

Daniel and Rogers write:

> The Church does not provide in-service training or graduate training in dealing with interpersonal stress or the interpersonal processes which provide the cleric with realistic goals and good self-understanding.[4]

The minister needs to develop real skills in the area of self-awareness and gift-awareness[5] in order to alleviate some of the avoidable stressors of the ministry.

Modelling

Your expectations of your church may come from what you have already experienced in other churches you have observed.

Love me

Love is a realistic expectation but is not immediate and may take on a different shape to your expectation, as with Jim in the case study above.

Follow me

It is not unusual for a leader simply to expect that the people will follow their lead because they are the designated leader. Leadership in a voluntary organisation, such as the church, may be designated but needs to take place at the level of your relationship with the people. If you see yourself in the shepherd's role and expect a flock to follow you, you will first need to show that you are a good shepherd and worthy of trust. Many leaders fall back on their ordination or designation in the mistaken thought that it will be enough. Leadership is earned! In many churches the congregation have seen a succession of ministers come and go, all with bright ideas, trends and projects. Lives have been tipped upside down and change has been so frequent that congregations have been left giddy with activity. Why should they follow you and your lead without developing trust through a period of getting to know you?

Learn from me
Many ministers understand their role as one of teacher. Their expectation is that the congregation will listen and learn. This can happen only if you can teach and communicate in such a way that people are able to listen. Many leaders are simply not good teachers or preachers and wonder why their ministry in this area seems to be struggling. As a leader, the responsibility is upon you to have something worth saying, and to say it well. For many, the ability to be a good communicator has not taken shape at theological college or ministry training school, and further work is needed. Having people listen and learn from you does not come with the designation or ordination.

Understand me
Many of my clients have expressed that they are in pain and that the reason for this is that their congregation seem to have little understanding when it comes to their own or their family needs. While it is by no means universally true, there can be a huge gulf between pastor and people when it comes to being understood. The ministry has been a well-kept secret in many settings, the minister being a kind of mythological being unlike other human beings.

Having served as a minister for thirteen years in my first church I had the following conversation. A young woman in the congregation said, 'Hi Colin, how are you doing today?' I wasn't feeling great, as I had some things on my mind, so I said, 'Oh, not too good today – too much to think about I guess!' She replied, 'Do you know it has never occurred to me that you may ever have any problems, you being a minister and all!' I was amazed that after so many years with them anyone could fail to recognise my humanity. Understanding is more likely to be achieved to some degree through an open and honest ministry that kills the myth of superhumanity and allows people to see you as no different from them.

Share my spirituality
One of the most common misconceptions is the thought that the whole congregation believes the same things about God, church, etc. A church with a corporate sense of direction, or that represents a particular churchmanship, is still a group of individuals who will have wide variance in what they believe. Leaders can become frustrated about this if they feel they are getting nowhere, or if they feel that the church is not behind

them. Leaders have often given up ministry for this very reason. I think it is far better to find out what people do believe and to enter into a period of in-depth teaching on spirituality. Generally I feel that there is a widespread marked lack of this kind of teaching. The development of thought and theology at a consumable level is a great asset.

Grasp my direction
As with the above, the assumption that a congregation is 'right there' with the leader's sense of direction and vision is often a mistake. A congregation will include a wide variety of personality types, many of whom do not work well with 'big picture' information. Vision needs to be imparted in bite-sized chunks for a large number of people. You may know what you mean and where you want to go, but church leadership requires that the people go too. Take more time and care with this and you will experience less frustration. Sometimes there can be a fear of change, a reluctance or even stubbornness on the part of some, but all too many leaders accuse the church of these things for want of a better and more thorough approach to this kind of leadership.

Communicating with a congregation is a skill. As with any relationship, messages have a habit of missing the mark and communication can be clumsy. If you expect too much from your congregation, you may blame them for your own mistakes or may even get hurt unintentionally.

Reflection

Reflect on this last section and ask yourself what you are expecting from your church. Do you feel that these expectations of yours are reasonable and well founded?

What does your church expect from your ministry? Expectations are levelled on church leaders from all congregations and church types. These often exceed the possibilities of any human being. E.B. Bratcher writes:

> The reasons for experiencing low self-esteem are numerous but can be expressed in one statement: the pastor is expected to 'walk on water' and he cannot, and he becomes angry with himself because he cannot.

> Dr Roger K. White, a psychiatrist who has counselled many ministers, stated that the minister is under constant pressure to accomplish far more than he is capable of doing. Some of the expectations that the average congregation has of its pastor are:
>
> 1. He must be a perfect moral example.
> 2. He must provide moral and emotional support at all times regardless of his own condition.
> 3. He must be an able administrator both in the church and in the community.
> 4. He must be an able public speaker on any and every topic.
> 5. He must perform, as an actor to keep people on the edge of their seats at all times, be able to act in all settings (for example, funerals, weddings, picnics, baptisms, etc.).
> 6. He must serve as a philosopher, a teacher of values, even though the people agree beforehand that they will not listen.
> 7. He must perform as a counselor, a role that is particularly emotionally exhausting.
>
> If any man could accomplish all of these tasks, he would also be able to walk on water.[6]

It is often the case that the Christian minister will try to please all of the people all of the time as a means of avoiding conflict and keeping the people happy. This motif can lead to an overburdened role that is likely to cause damage to the health of the minister as well as to their family and ultimately to the church that they serve.

Perceived expectations, which are frequently the cause of low self-esteem, can be crippling to the work of Christian ministers. Much of the work is self-motivated and self-monitored and they often do not know what to tackle first, since whatever they do seems to make little difference to the mountain of work remaining.

This is a list of what ministers commonly perceive they are expected to be. I have drawn it from a wide group of serving Christian ministers who have come through my counselling service over the last five years. Most of these expectations were communicated to them formally by their church or individually by church members:

- God
- God, once removed (the nearest person to God)
- Perfect moral example
- Mighty warrior of faith and power
- Problem-solver (someone with all the answers)
- Hero of the faith
- Provider of support regardless of personal needs
- Listening ear
- Excellent administrator
- Shepherd
- Experienced counsellor
- Best friend
- Excellent communicator
- Knowledgeable in all subjects
- Bible expert
- Teacher

Even allowing for the first one as not altogether serious, the person able to fulfil all of these expectations would indeed be superhuman.

Developing your self-awareness can include learning about your strengths, weaknesses and gifts in ministry. Communicating with your church about who and what you are can help to bring greater reality into the expectations a church may have of you.

Contract negotiation (recognising that some church types have a non-negotiable fixed understanding of the role of minister) can be a great help in all of this where it is possible. I have been criticised for this suggestion by those ministers who consider their role to be a non-negotiable, divine appointment that is biblically defined and not able to be changed. However, learning to work according to your gifts and personality will often lead to a better job being done and a healthier experience of the ministry for all concerned. Knowing who you are and what you can do will help prospective churches to employ you more realistically.

Learning to say no, rather than a very frequent yes, can help a church to recognise that you are one person and unable to please all of the people all of the time, or to undertake tasks that require more than one person. Developing assertiveness skills can mean that healthier communication can take place.

Reflection

Do you say yes to every request made by the church? Are you able to work within your skill base?

What are you expecting from God?

Our understanding of God differs from person to person, based on a wide range of factors. It is certain that those of you reading this book will have varying ideas of God and His interaction with humanity. Consequently you will also differ in what you may be expecting from Him.

Jim, from the case study earlier, expected that God would back him up and make things happen. He was surprised, even shocked, to discover that God did not instantly make things right. Jim was a 'minister of the gospel'. If God didn't work this way for Jim and other ministers, then what chance had the rest of the church?

Jim had formed the opinion that God was required to work according to the will of those who serve Him. He would never have put it quite this way but it amounts to the same thing. Just sometimes we endeavour to create God in our own image. It would not be exaggerating to say that a form of polytheism exists within the Church at large: we have a tendency to shape God and our understanding of Him according to our own needs and hopes. Consequently there will be many god-types that we believe are God. The fact is that He, and not you or I, is God. He has his own unfathomable ways.

Henri J.M. Nouwen, in his book *Intimacy: Essays in Pastoral Psychology* addresses this point in the section called 'From magic to faith'.[7] Nouwen points out that sometimes we expect the same magic from God today in adult life that we expected as infants when we cried out for food and it appeared. Infants easily develop the thought that simply wanting something and expressing it loudly enough will result in its provision. This is the 'Father Christmas' approach to God, which fails to take stock of any theology of suffering. It fails to understand how God builds character into his people, and is lacking in its ability to sustain difficulty and hardship. The ministering person with this approach will inevitably find ministry life difficult to survive. This is moving from God as 'provider', to God the source of 'supply on demand'.

How we view God will determine our expectations of Him! Some of the clients I have worked with have become distant from and disappointed with God, largely because He has not functioned according to their understanding. If you believe in a God who will never allow you to suffer, what happens when you are suffering? What do you do if heaven seems silent when you are asking for specific guidance? It is not untypical to hear ministers making convoluted apologies and arguments to explain why God has not acted in certain ways and circumstances, when a more informed theology would be helpful.

As a leader, you need to reflect regularly on the nature of God and His interface with humankind; to develop realistic expectations that strengthen your walk with Him. Second-hand belief systems lead to first-hand pain.

Reflection

What do I believe about God? What do I expect from Him? What do I think about guidance, suffering, protection and provision?

What are you expecting from your spouse?

It would be a mistake to jump this section if you are currently single, as it is possible that you may yet marry. If you are a ministering person now, or at sometime in the future, then it is certain you will need to consider the marriage relationship.

In our last case study, Jim Mortlake had laid an expectation upon his wife that as part of the call to ministry she would fall into line unquestioningly behind him. Jim had made vast assumptions:

- He had believed that his wife had the same commitment to the ministering role as himself.
- He had believed that his wife could be left for long periods over many months and that this would not affect their relationship because they were 'about the Lord's work'.
- He had expected his wife to believe that the sacrifice of relationship in the name of ministry was the right thing and that she both understood and was happy with it.

- Jim had expected his wife's life to cease to exist as an entity as it was swallowed up by their joint call to ministry.

This is not to suggest that God does not call both partners to the ministry. It is inevitable that as long as the professional, vocational ministry exists, couples and indeed families will move to the place of service often many miles from their familiar surroundings. I am sure that God considers the unit and not just the individual when He places His ministers and servants wherever He chooses. The problems that occur are more to do with the expectations laid on the spouse by the minister/partner, the church and themselves. Statistics suggest that an increasing number of ministry marriages are either breaking or are at serious risk of doing so. Ministering couples in counselling frequently outline the kind of issues Jim faced.

Consider these possibilities for the minister's spouse. They must:

- Run the ladies'/men's group in the church
- Visit the 'shut-ins' and those whom the minister cannot get around to seeing
- Be an excellent host/hostess
- Act as an unpaid curate/associate pastor
- Answer all calls at the house and protect the minister from being disturbed
- Attend *all* church functions as a picture of warmth and congeniality
- Perform secretarial duties for the minister

The list could go on. However, it can be seen clearly that the minister's spouse may be called on to undertake a wide range of activities. Many believe that their own lives have withered away in the face of overwhelming expectations. They feel an inability to express their own needs in the face of the call to ministry until they are in personal crisis, and then it is expressed with a passion.

The church's expectations of your spouse are worthy of consideration, but what are you expecting (or would you expect) of your spouse? For some ministers the spouse is 'the ministry on view', an inseparable aspect of their own ministry, and so they expect the spouse to act accordingly and not let the side down!

Reflection

Are your expectations here reasonable and well-founded? Reflect on this section with your spouse and find out their feelings.

What are you expecting from your children?

In a later section of this book we will consider the experiences of children of ministering persons. Here we are looking at expectations that ministering persons put on their children.

For example, Jenny Peterson is the thirteen-year-old daughter of the local vicar. She is beginning to find it difficult to go to church and is embarrassed to be at the local school. She is beginning to feel like a freak in her society. What could be the cause of this?

There really are immense expectations put on the children of ministers from different sources:

- The parents
- The church
- The local community
- Other ministering persons in the area
- Local children

Perhaps a more pertinent question here would be, 'What are you expecting from your children?' Like the spouse, children can be seen as an extension of the minister's public image and as such need to keep it untarnished. What follows is a typical list of expectations levelled at the children of Christian leaders. They must:

- Keep up appearances and not let the ministry down in the eyes of the church
- Make the minister look like a good parent in the eyes of the church
- Behave better than any other children in the church
- Be high achievers at school
- Be quiet, considerate people and not be the cause of embarrassment
- Always be smartly dressed
- Always remember their manners

- Share their parents with all the church
- Spend long hours without their parents without complaint or ill effect
- Share their homes with all the church and must therefore go to their rooms when meetings are being held
- Not want more than the ministry salary could possibly afford, and rise above the wants of their peers
- Be more interested in God and the church than any other child in the church
- Be able to answer the questions put to the Sunday-school class

This is a huge list of demands for any child to meet.

Reflection

This requires a good deal of honesty and soul-searching on your part, but what do you expect of your children (if you have them) and is it reasonable? Are there any adjustments or apologies to be made?

Perhaps the best expectation we can place on any child is that they simply be a child, look like a child and think like a child! Children cannot be asked to contribute to the public face of the ministering person. Many ministers suffer great stresses from living on their persona, and should not be asking their children to do the same.

What are the expectations God has of *you*?

We have seen that ministers may have expectations of themselves that are exaggerated and impossible. We have also seen that they may have unrealistic expectations of God.

Reflection

Think briefly for a moment about the expectations that you feel God has of you. What do you believe He expects from your ministry? Are your perceived expectations reasonable? Do they fit the thinking generated by this section of the book so far?

Our understanding of the nature of God is much involved here. It is suggestive of the parable of the talents and what the recipients of responsibilities believed of their master – their perceived expectations! If you are ministering out of a sense of paying God back for His goodness towards you, or out of a sense of guilt with a desire to appease the Deity, then you will quite likely develop an unhealthy 'drivenness' to your work, called by some 'workaholism'. It is important that we think carefully about God's expectations of us, but also to realise that 'As a father has compassion on his children, so the LORD has compassion on those who fear him; for he knows how we are formed, he remembers that we are dust' (Psa. 103:13–14).

God knows us and His expectations are founded in understanding our being: 'My frame was not hidden from you when I was made in the secret place. When I was woven together in the depths of the earth …' (Psa. 139:15).

Reflection

Are your responses in the service of God congruent with your understanding of His nature?

Amazingly, ministers preach a God of peace and control, while 'burning out' in stress frenzies that belie what they espouse. This lack of congruence is observable not only by spouse and family but also by the church they serve and the world they seek to save. Ministries that reflect the essence of their belief system are necessary for the mission of the Church today.

This chapter encourages readers to consider their understanding of expectations from a number of perspectives. It points to the real need for an honest approach to ministry, and suggests that you think hard and look deeply at expectations.

Ministers should consider re-evaluating their role every six months, effectively 'checking themselves'. Consider the following checklist:

- Am I still working according to my sense of call?
- Am I working in line with my gifts and strengths?
- Am I working with a healthy set of personal expectations?

- Am I working with a healthy set of expectations of my spouse?
- Am I working with a healthy set of expectations of my children?
- Am I working with a healthy set of expectations of my church?
- Am I working with a healthy set of expectations of my God?
- Am I working too long and too hard?
- Am I taking a healthy amount of time off?
- Am I frustrated by anything at present?

If a negative answer is found at any point on the list, then your work is clear: find out what is happening and try to change it.

Ministers may wish to have their work assessed by their church/employers once a year. This provides an opportunity to reflect on what they do or are perceived to do and how effective they are. It is a talking point and provides the much-needed opportunity for communication. The ministering person may wish to find a trusted colleague who could act as a mentor and provide valuable feedback to some of the questions.

Our theology will dictate how we interpret both call and the expectations that come with it. If self-awareness can be a skill that will alleviate ministry stress, then God-awareness and congruent working practices will also have this effect.

5. Power, Authority and the Ministry

I answered the telephone recently to hear a young woman with a friendly voice offering me a bargain if I wanted to buy a mobile phone. She told me how wonderful the deal was and that it could not be beaten. I said that I was interested but would need to see the specifications of the phone and view the national coverage of the network. The young woman gave me scant details and I asked for more information in writing. It was then that I learned that the offer was a 'here and now, there and then' deal. Order now in this moment or lose the deal! Not given to instant financial decisions, I refused the offer. It nagged at me and for a while I wondered if I had made a mistake. On reflection I realised that I had been given the 'pressure sales' treatment. The power of the 'great deal' had been held over me and I had been expected to give in and buy. I have encountered this approach scores of times and rarely respond, but perhaps (at worst) because of human greed or (at best) curiosity, I often wonder what I have missed out on. I am a victim of power dynamics at play through telephone sales.

We are bombarded with power play every day of our lives: 'Do this; don't do that; buy now; send no money for fourteen days.' Many of us suppose we are immune to the influence of power dynamics, but we are mistaken. Subtle selling techniques are employed to draw us all in through smells, tastes, sounds, colours, touch, etc. Many organisations have learned that human beings respond to an array of techniques with our vastly differing learning approaches, and information is presented as a broadside to have maximum impact. While I consider this to be highly manipulative, I recognise that it is a business ploy and that financial success is important for the future of any company. So I bow to the inevitable in the commercial world; but what about the world of the Church? Should we expect the Church to be a pressure-free zone? Well, whatever we might expect, wherever there are people there are power dynamics at play.

Power and authority are linked dynamics that curse and bless each other with regularity. Christian ministers in any church setting involve themselves with power dynamics, regardless of their church type or system of church government. Wherever one person holds out their hand to another, power comes into play. When one person leads another across a busy road, there is a leader and a follower. It is impossible to develop a system that is 'power free'.

The word 'power', in this regard, tends to have negative connotations, as many people are able to recall personal experiences or well-known stories where power has been misused. Power is really describing a force or an energy that can be used positively for the good of all concerned. There is no escaping from power dynamics in all walks of life.

This chapter will consider power and authority in the light of the Church and its leaders. I will endeavour to describe the nature of power in the ministry and consider the handling of this force in such a way that it is most positive for all concerned.

What is really going on? There are many church types and expressions of local church. Let me take one as an example, say, the Baptist Church, and demonstrate by way of introduction how power can vary even in defined power systems. Baptists are governed, as independent churches, by the 'church meeting'. This supposedly gives 'power' to the people and alleviates any possible misuse of power by a minister, since he or she is accountable to the church meeting. This also prevents, in theory, any other individual from dominating the church by their personality. In reality, however, there are a number of possibilities:

- If the minister has a persuasive style, many may be swayed by what he or she has to say and will 'vote' with the minister. This is power with the minister.
- There could be an individual or a family who have been long established in the local church. It is possible that this family may hold strong influence in the church and that people will vote with them. This is power with a family.
- One church member may be eloquent and passionate whenever speaking in a church meeting and people could be persuaded by the power of this well-presented argument and vote accordingly. It is highly likely that many church members are not exposed to the competitiveness of debate in any other place in their lives apart from the church meeting and are thus persuaded. This is power with the individual.

This is not intended as a critique of the Baptist Church's governmental style but as an illustration of the ways that power and authority can operate in circumstances where a system has within its design the possibility of factors beyond its control. It is impossible to have any organisation, church or otherwise, that is fully in control of its 'power factors'.

Towards an understanding of power

There are power dynamics at work, almost without us realising it, in everyday behaviour, such as crossing the street when the little green man appears on the traffic light. Or in keeping right on the escalator. Or only eight persons being allowed in the lift at the department store. Or not walking on the grass in the park. Or a sign not to touch wet paint. The last example seems almost to be a challenge to do just the opposite. Many people find it difficult to resist touching the paintwork to see if what the sign says is true.

My task is not so much to illustrate all the points of contact with power and authority in our lives as to see the impact of this in the work of the Christian minister.

And God said ...

Christian ministers believe that there is an aspect of the supernatural in their work and this often takes the form of a sense of 'divine involvement' in all that they do in the life of the church. They have a sense of God in their work, which is wonderful, but it can go sadly wrong!

Christian ministers need to have a strong sense of integrity to handle this power dynamic. They have within their grasp a powerful tool indeed. They may believe that everything they do or say comes directly from God's mouth, and may begin to operate with a sense of infallibility, because they believe that they are endued with divine power and authority. Some ministering persons lose contact with their own humanity and fallibility.

Case study

Bill lasted just two years as pastor of his first church. He had started pastoring immediately after he had left theological college, with a strong sense of God and all that was about to happen. He 'knew' that God had His hand on his life and this meant that they were all, pastor and congregation, about to take a journey together that would lead to great blessing and church growth.

Things went well to begin with. The church appeared to be motivated by the changes that had taken place and with the calling of their new minister. His enthusiasm seemed to carry them along like a whirlwind.

Bill became overconfident, however, and began to implement changes to the nature of the fellowship that were too profound to happen overnight. One church member, followed by a few others, expressed to Bill that they were unhappy with things changing so fast and wanted more teaching and more of an explanation for what was taking place among them.

Bill saw this as a challenge to his authority. He was called of God and enabled by Him. His authority came from God and as such he was not to be questioned about the direction of the church. Once or twice Bill said, 'If you don't agree with me, then you are disobedient to God.'

Within a month the church was split down the middle. Half the members believed that they had in their midst a man of God, not to be questioned, while others felt that it was unreasonable to take such a stance. All they had wanted was further help with the possible changes. They felt pressurised and dealt with by a heavy hand.

Two months later, Bill was asked to leave the church; he left and took a handful of church members with him. He was unable to see that he had made some obvious mistakes in handling people. He had been 'standing' on his belief that he was hearing from God as 'the man of God' and should not be questioned.

Bill had started well but fell into the trap of considering himself more highly than he ought:

> For by the grace given me I say to every one of you: Do not think of yourself more highly than you ought, but rather think of yourself with sober judgment, in accordance with the measure of faith God has given you. (Rom. 12:3)

Bill's story is not uncommon. Falling back on what 'God says' can be a protective scheme used by leaders when they feel insecure in what they are doing or saying and if they fear the challenge of influential people. Using the name of God to give extra weight to a viewpoint is also a power technique employed by leaders (sometimes unconsciously) when they want to get their viewpoint across most strongly. Ministry can become dangerous and fleshly when spiritual authority is abused and undue manipulation is applied.

Reflection

Do you agree with this assessment of Bill? Reflect on your views here.

Power imbalance

Spiritual authority can often be claimed by Christian ministers on the basis that they have been called to God's service. Spiritual authority can be 'awarded' to Christian ministers also on the basis not only that they have been called by God but also that their call has been recognised by many, including the denominational officials where appropriate, and by the congregation. This is like a seal of approval and is often good for many years, valued nationally and internationally depending on your church type. This is reasonable and is the belief of many when it comes to calling a minister to a church. Some, however, feel intensely this presence of a 'man or woman of God'. They are overawed and look up to their pastor or minister as the voice of God.

This can put a great deal of pressure on Christian ministers and can lead them into difficulty. When the members of the congregation look up to their minister they can also look down upon themselves and award great authority to this person. A power imbalance is experienced (probably unavoidably so) that places huge responsibility on the minister to use this dynamic for the glory of God and for the good of the congregation. This can be difficult to handle and requires a good deal of honesty and self-awareness. The unscrupulous minister could exploit this form of hero worship for personal gain, which has happened on a number of occasions.

Case study

The Revd G.G. Brown and his Revivals Incorporated urged the congregation, in an emotionally charged atmosphere, to give all that they had to the offering. This was taking place in an inner-city area where financial deprivation was high. A number of members of the congregation, with great shows of emotion, emptied their wallets and purses.

A group of schoolboys put in their pocket money and were called to the front and interviewed. 'Did you boys put in all that you had?' 'We did.' 'Where did you get your money, boys?' 'It was our pocket money that we pooled together.' 'Did you hear that folks? These boys gave their pocket money to the work of the Lord.'

The collection continued and much fuss was made when a bus conductor who came to the meeting straight from work placed his unopened wage packet into the offering regardless of the consequences for his dependants. The belief was that God was going to honour this giving because the Revd G.G. Brown had said so.

This is a true story. Some days later the schoolboys reflected on these events and considered that they had been carried along by the emotion of the meeting and the methods of the minister. They felt that they had been used. Two of the boys questioned the integrity of Christianity as the result of this, and in their youth gave up their new-found faith in God.

Most abuses of power are not so clear as the story above. The learning curve here is not that you have just heard the best arguments against the abuse of power in the world, but that you are thinking about how you lead and what power motifs you may adopt in your ministry.

Reflection

Do you realise how powerful your position may be to the people in your congregation? What incidents of abuse of ministry power are you aware of in your experience? Consider how your leadership style might lead to the temptation to abuse your position.

Power tools

At different times throughout the past one hundred years, the media have reported numerous misuses of power. During the 1990s a number of high-profile cases on television and in the printed news have revealed manipulative practices. There is a need for leadership in all walks of life, but human insecurity often means that people want to opt out of decision-making and responsibility and leave it to the leaders. In my counselling practice, many clients begin their counselling by communicating a need to be told what to do by me: 'I am in need and don't know what to do; will you get me out of this?' Some Christian ministers have exploited this need and have become powerful, and sometimes wealthy, as the result of this ministry motif.

Although there are incidents of deliberate power misuse or malpractice, it is important to note that power may be misused and people may be manipulated without Christian ministers realising they are doing this. Many have adopted types of ministry from others who have become powerful role models. What follows is a descriptive list of some of the 'power tools' that may be employed in the ministry:

Power dressing

Dressing in clothes that create a sense of presence and authority, clothing not usually worn by other members of the church, which often draws attention to yourself and not to God. (This may of course be required or expected by your church tradition.)

Power speak

Using volume to get your point across, with over-dramatic presentation; working the microphone to create emotional swings in the congregation; frequent use of the words 'submit' and 'obey' when referring to an office held in the church.

Emotionalism

Emotion may naturally play a part in worship, as coming close to God can be deeply emotional. This tool is used when a Christian minister plays on the emotions of the congregation with the raising and lowering of the voice, the use of crocodile tears and the frequent use of emotive stories.

'God says...' or 'God told me ...'
This is not a reference to the reading of Scripture but to the validation of a point being made by the Christian minister. This is the same as saying, 'You can't argue with this; it comes straight from God.' This leaves no room for discussion and is highly confrontational.

Gang-building
This is where Christian ministers gather a group of 'yes' people around them to protect and agree with their points of view and acts of leadership – another form of power play.

Lying
This includes the use of half-truths and decorated truth employed by Christian ministers when they feel threatened and caught out in their behaviour or with their failure to carry out certain tasks. No one expects the Christian minister to lie and the Christian minister understands this when they lie to get out of trouble.

Exaggeration
Like lying, this is embellishing the truth. Often used when trying to impress the congregation or colleagues; for example: 'I always get up at 5.00am to pray for you all.' The truth is: 'I have twice in the last six months got up at 6.00am to pray and fell asleep while doing it.' The Christian minister who feels the need to impress employs this motif and it is often coupled with a low sense of self-worth. Many people can tell when a Christian minister is exaggerating and Christian ministers are often caught out.

Name-dropping
The same as exaggeration. This is the need to impress when you do not feel impressive. Sometimes employed by those who are comparing their ministries with other 'well-known names', always as the result of a sense of inadequacy.

Atmospherics
I mean by this, Christian ministers who create an atmosphere around them of distance and rank. Like the Christian minister who sits behind a huge desk when people come into their office to have a pastoral discus-

sion, or the minister who is afraid to get too near to the people for fear of being discovered as a fraud, weak, or in need, etc.

Public correction
This is the minister who often corrects people's behaviour in public. This is a form of humiliation and carries the message, 'I am righteous and you are not.'

Binding members
This refers to the practice of the Christian minister who makes it difficult for the church members ever to leave the church. Some have gone as far as to suggest that terrible things will happen if the person leaves, since 'God has said' that they should remain. This is a position of fear that says, 'If I don't bind the people then they will leave, because I am not a good enough minister to hold them.'

Heroic stance
This is where the ministers frequently tell stories of their great deeds done in the service of the Lord. The emphasis always points to the greatness of the doer. This is PR work and is connected with low self-worth. When ministers feel the need to advertise their own greatness the emphasis has slipped from bringing glory to God, to glorifying self. This a common trait.

The above is not offered as a complete list. As I read again the list I have written I am aware that these motifs are in common use and are not so easily identified. I am aware that there have been times in my years as a minister that I have used more than one of these power tools, particularly when I have been at my most vulnerable and insecure. Not that I set out to use the tools to fend off others, but I simply slid neatly into using them without so much as a second thought. In my journey of personal growth as a leader, I am aware of a good many mistakes I have made along the way and I hope and pray that giving them recognition enables me to deal with my needs in a better way.

I am sure that as you look through the power tools list you can spot people whom you know or have heard of before. Difficult though this may be, take a second look and think about your own ministry motifs both now and in the past.

Reflection

Where do you see yourself in the list? Are there better ways of coping with your own need than using a set of power tools?

Other ministry motifs

- 'Hundreds die as religious leader declares suicide to be the only answer.'
- 'Religious leader declares that he will not be seen in public again until his followers have raised £1,000,000.'
- 'Religious leader forbids marriage.'
- 'Religious leader controls lives. Many give up their homes, money and belongings for the cause.'

Headlines like these appear frequently in the press and on our televisions. Although many ministering persons know how to use their position positively to the glory of God, behave wisely in their use of 'awarded authority', and take care to value the people whom they serve, some clearly do not. Often the misuse of power and authority stems from a driving or motivational force within.

As we consider the subject of power and authority, we look next at some of the types of leadership that are at large. I will endeavour to look at the motivation for the ministry type adopted. While the examples are a little simplistic, they are offered in such a way as to make them more easily recognisable. In real-life situations the motif may be as simple as the examples below, but offered with a measure of camouflage.

'I am a man or woman of God, therefore I cannot be questioned'

This is the position outlined in our case study about Bill, and can be understood as a position of fear. Those who hold to this point of view as a ministry type may well be hiding behind their office. They may feel a sense of inadequacy for the tasks they carry out and so hope to get through by a display of authority. These people are frequently heard reminding the church of the office they hold:

- 'As your minister I …'
- 'My office among you requires that …'
- 'Must I remind you that I am a man of God …?'

It is difficult for these kind of leaders to 'hear' any helpful correctives on their approach to their work. Although it is true to say that all Christian people are men and women of God, this motif encourages the 'elite' view of ministry and suggests that the people are in a different spiritual place, of lesser importance, to the minister. This encourages a hierarchical view of church life and leads to others looking for significance through promotion in the leadership structure of the church.

'I am a servant of the people'

This type of ministry is at one level balanced and helpful. It is a position of heart. At all times those working in Christian ministry need to see themselves as servants of God. However, it can also be interpreted as a position of weakness where the Christian minister takes no leadership role and simply becomes the 'do-gooder' who is always available. Here a minister can look for worth from the 'feel-good factor' that may (although not always) come from people who consider their minister as always available to help. This can amount to a denial of the minister's own and family needs in order to hear that he or she is doing well. Where there is a measure of weakness here, it is possible that a stronger personality may emerge and threaten the leadership balance of the church. Such a motif will work well, however, if the minister finds worth from sources other than the acclaim of the congregation.

'I keep my head down'

This is a position of fear. A Christian minister may become fearful of dealing with the many conflicts that arise in any church. Wherever there are groups of people gathered, there are usually measures of conflict, particularly if leadership has moved from function to elitism. The Christian minister is frequently required to intervene and this intervention is emotionally costly. Responsible leadership can bring high stress factors and none more so than with the conflict resolution mode. Many personality types seek to avoid conflict by ducking the issues, particularly since engaging in this task can bring blame to the peacemaker for interfering. Since this is uncomfortable for Christian ministers, they may have developed the defence mechanism of hiding. Some Christian ministers will literally avoid people in the street or the church building if they feel this will entangle them in a difficult situation. Avoiding the issues often leads to greater destruction taking place in the church community, so hiding may indeed make things worse.

'I cannot be held responsible'

Like the last point, this is a position of fear, the fear that the minister may be blamed for a set of circumstances that has arisen. It is a position of hiding that believes, 'If it's nothing to do with me then I cannot be held responsible.' It is possible that such a motif may stem from childhood where making mistakes led to harsh disciplinary measures. Ultimately, this motif results in failure to take responsibility and fulfil a leadership role. It may also stem from an experience of being 'burned out': becoming worn down after a long period of conducting the ministry with an over-developed sense of responsibility. Energy levels can reach such a low ebb that any responsibility becomes an emotional and physical drain. This motif results in manipulative behaviour where Christian ministers seek to extract themselves from difficult situations.

'I'll show them who is boss!'

This is a position of anger, with pride probably lurking beneath the surface. It is indicative of people who feel trodden down, for whatever reason; who need to pull themselves up to their full height and strike back to prove their worth. We may see the 'I know what I'm talking about' heart or the 'They haven't the faintest idea what they're doing' heart. As we look deeper we will discover a form of anger causing this low sense of self-worth. Once again, childhood issues may be the root cause. Perhaps such people feel pressed down in life and now intend to redress the balance on the unsuspecting church that has called them. This is a dangerous position for the individual and the church, and usually leads to pain and disaster.

'Everything is great – do what makes you feel happy'

These people are usually good to be around for a while. They can have the appearance of freeing others to do what they are good at. They can give people a sense of security in that 'all is well'. Sometimes, however, the driving force behind this model or style of ministry is one of avoidance of responsibility. Actually, this motif ducks the issue of the need for certain guidelines and boundaries for church life. Such boundaries bring order and peace and help to avoid conflict. Freedom becomes anarchy when there are no boundaries to delineate acceptable from unacceptable behaviour. The real issue here may be one of fearing responsibility or feeling incapable of the task to which ministers have been called. Quite possibly they are abandoning their role within the church.

'I am going to build the biggest church for miles around'

This can be confusing even for the owner of the statement. Many good leaders have confused the building up of the church with establishing their own importance and esteem. Some Christian ministers are unaware that their desire for a larger church has much to do with their own desire to be successful and influential. Of course there can be a healthy desire for church growth and for a greater impact on the community around, but such a desire to succeed probably comes from the 'need to succeed'. Success is not to be despised, but a drivenness to succeed in such a way that others need to acknowledge it usually comes from a place of wounding. Many of these people grew up in a success-based society, recognising that their parents wanted them to do well and be seen to do well at school and in life. Unfortunately some could never earn the approval of those who mattered most and so are driven to chase the wind, to strive continually for success without a tangible, measurable target. Churches will never grow fast enough or large enough to silence the inner voice that haunts leaders such as these.

For about my first five years as a minister I played the 'numbers game'; I would count the number of people in my congregation and be pleased when there were many and not so pleased when there were fewer than before. I told myself that I was simply interested in church growth dynamics, when in truth I wanted the sweet taste of success. Success for me, that is! I wanted to be the minister of a fast-track, fast-growing church that reflected me. I struggled with the rights and wrongs of all of this until I realised that I could get no higher in my life than I had already reached. I was and am a child of God from where there is no meaningful promotion. There came a point for me where I felt rebuked by God for believing in my ability rather than His to build the church. This may not be true for you, but it was for me, and I eventually stopped counting heads.

I am tempted now to offer you the motif that is most healthy and productive, but in reality no such model exists. There can be only right attitudes and helpful approaches, all of which spring from a spiritually and emotionally healthy lifestyle. Such a lifestyle can be neither bought nor copied but develops over time in individuals who are prepared to be travellers or eternal students in the journey of life with God, remaining in touch with their humanity.

If you see something of yourself in some of these motifs (and you probably will) then simply acknowledge what you see. Self-awareness can be shocking at times when we make unpleasant discoveries about our motives for what we do or say. Thankfully, God is full of grace and allows us to grow. He will help us to move from where we are, to better and more informed methods of ministry.

Reflection

What feelings has this section allowed to surface? Can you see yourself in any of this?

Power and character

A few years ago some colleagues and I hosted a series of one-day conferences for Christian leaders at a well-known London conference centre. The first two were a great success. A list of well-known speakers and a topical subject seemed to be the winning formula. Around 1,500 leaders attended each conference. The third was at the same place with the same formula, except for one change – the subject. We had decided, as conference organisers, that one of the most pressing needs among leaders was the development of integrity. We set the topic and posted the invitations but, when the day came, only 150 delegates attended. When we went on to hold a fourth conference on another topical subject, however, there was a huge turnout. Integrity seems to be a thorny subject for leaders!

Character and integrity are the great safeguards and health-giving boundaries to the use of power and authority. World history cries out with horrific stories when character and integrity are absent. Millions have lost their lives over the centuries thanks to unscrupulous leaders. Thank God for His Church where peace reigns and where leaders demonstrate leadership integrity that should be the envy of the world. Like a light in the darkness Christian leadership points the way to the correct use of power for the world.

Probably one of the biggest problems with the use of power is that many Christian leaders have not considered their power motif or level of integrity, and many have held back from the process of personal growth that leads to inner security and peace. When Jesus said, 'Peace I leave with you; my peace I give you. I do not give to you as the world gives. Do not let your hearts be troubled and do not be afraid' (John 14:27), He was speaking of a deep-rooted, heart–mind dynamic that is the envy of the world. Leaders often work out their role with an insecurity that impedes their use of power and authority, and colours their leadership. If we can sort out a disintegrated belief system, then leadership from the place of peace will flourish. We can preach 'peace', but living with it is harder to do. Our belief systems and lifestyles need to become an integrated whole.

This may be an uncomfortable topic for you as you read it and you may already have decided that I make too many generalisations with my use of 'many'. However, my perspectives come from much research and from years of working on myself and with other leaders in searching for a better personal perspective. I have always been impressed with the way that Jesus was able to handle His critics. There was not a hint of insecurity to be found when mocked and accused. It seems as though He was so fully aware of who He was and of His standing with His Father that no amount of name-calling or false accusations could convince Him otherwise: 'Do what you like to Me and say what you like, I am still the Son of God.' For me, Jesus is our model of Christian maturity and peace. Christlikeness is maturity, bringing an inner security that acknowledges that we cannot reach any higher than 'sonship'. Acceptance of ourselves with all our strengths and weaknesses, in the knowledge that we are His, and through Christ made acceptable to Him, is a route to deep security and peace from which may spring true altruistic leadership and use of power. This can lead to a healthy, safe self-evaluation that can enhance our leadership skills and use of the power and authority such roles engender.

I am unconvinced that our growth in maturity leads to a total sense of security or that we *can* ever feel totally secure in this world. However, we can make significant life-changing and peace-bringing advances in this area.

Reflection

What has this section of the chapter made you feel? Are you aware of areas of insecurity in your life and ministry, and can you list them? If you can, are you able to reflect on the kind of leadership behaviour this has brought about in you?

The following exercise requires a good deal of honesty and courage to reflect. It is a little self-test but *beware*! Self-tests are not the final word on you and cannot see into your inner being. At best, they are helpful indicators.

I have designed this test, which I call the 'I' test, as a simple procedure to help you discover the measure of the insecurity that you may experience with your role. You can beat the test and get around it. You can argue with its scientific value and point to its flaws, of which I am sure there are many. Or, you can take it honestly, and use the information for personal growth. Few of us will have a zero score. A high percentage does not indicate that you are unfit to lead; the test simply acknowledges feelings of insecurity that you can work on for the future.

The 'I' Test

Place a tick to the left of the statements in this list that are true, regardless of how strongly so. Do the test quickly without dwelling on any question for very long.

1. I need to be loved by everyone.
2. I need to please the people.
3. I need not to be discovered for who I really am.
4. If only they knew what went on in my mind.
5. I need to be the best.
6. I need to be seen.
7. I need to be heard.
8. I need to have attention.
9. I need to have the biggest church.
10. I need the best income.

11. I need to pretend.
12. I need to do it all myself.
13. I am uncomfortable if someone questions my motives.
14. I frequently feel attacked by the people.
15. I wish people would take notice of what I say.
16. I feel vulnerable.
17. I am in pain.
18. I must protect myself.
19. I must make them see my strengths.
20. I must make them see what I know.
21. I must be seen to be mature.
22. I must be more mature than they are.
23. I must know more than they do.
24. I must be an expert.
25. No one listens to me.
26. No one knows who I really am.
27. No one cares for me.
28. No one understands me.
29. No one can help me.
30. I am not sure that I am intelligent enough.
31. I am not sure that I know enough.
32. I am not sure that I believe what I say.
33. I am not sure that I say what I believe.

(a) Add up the number of statements that are true for you and multiply by three for your 'I' percentage. The higher your percentage, the greater your feelings of insecurity are likely to be.
(b) Whatever your score, make a list of the statements that reflect some of your insecurity, think through the causes, and reflect on what might help you to change this feeling.
(c) For the truly brave: ask a trusted other, spouse, friend, etc., to mark this test from their perspective of 'you' and discuss your findings together.

If you know, either with the help of the 'I' test or from general self-awareness, that you suffer from medium to high levels of insecurity, then you may want to opt for a period of professional counselling and reflection to enable you to grow in security. You will discover later in this book that I believe that counselling is a tool for the wise. Obtaining professional help to enable us to reflect on our lives is a mature thing to do and I strongly encourage Christian leaders to opt for regular periods of counselling as a commitment to personal growth.

The best leadership power motif

The desire to see God's Church built up needs to be the central driving force behind Christian leadership. It is a desire to engage in ministry in such a way that God receives the glory and the Church is equipped. This represents freedom from the fear and insecurity that makes many leadership decisions self-focused, and enables the leader to look outwards. Consider the following passages:

> This is why I write these things when I am absent, that when I come I may not have to be harsh in my use of authority – the authority the Lord gave me for building you up, not for tearing you down. (2 Cor. 13:10)

> It was he who gave some to be apostles, some to be prophets, some to be evangelists, and some to be pastors and teachers, to prepare God's people for works of service, so that the body of Christ may be built up until we all reach unity in the faith and in the knowledge of the Son of God and become mature, attaining to the whole measure of the fulness of Christ. (Eph. 4:11–13)

Good Christian leadership, then, requires an empowering mentality along with good character. Christian ministers are people who have been awarded levels of responsibility that contain a measure of power and authority. Ministers often stand at the front of the church building and participate in the conducting of worship. They often lead groups and act as chairpersons of meetings. They are seen in the public eye to be in authority and are considered by the community to be respectable figures. The power and authority they have, which could lead them into potentially abusive situations, may be put to good use in the church and community. They may use their position to bless the church and enable people to mature in their walk with God. They may be effective in making changes in the local community that will benefit all through escaping the self-focused agenda.

6. Family Life and the Pressures of Ministry

Case study

Peter, the pastor of an independent church, told me a story about his family life and their experience of the church. On the day when the church elders had interviewed Peter, they had shown him the house that would be his to use if he were to be appointed as their next pastor. It was a nice enough house, but it had a curious privet bush, some six feet tall, three feet deep and four feet long. It stood out in the garden like an obelisk with no apparent relationship to anything else. Peter observed the bush and ventured a question about its existence. He was told that it had been planted there to prevent a nosy church member in a house across the street from looking into the pastor's lounge window with a pair of binoculars. Peter shrugged it off then, but now realises that it was a portent of things to come. He was elected to the pastorate and eagerly began his ministry. The family moved into the house and at first was quite happy, even with the large bush immediately outside the lounge window.

As the months passed, Peter and his wife Mary had a number of odd experiences. Mary once had her washing criticised for not looking white enough, and another time for leaving it out on a Sunday. Peter was told by a senior elder that he was letting the side down by allowing the front lawn to get too long before he trimmed it. The children were told not to play outside for fear of disturbing the neighbours and so being a bad witness. Mary had her shopping bag inspected by an elder's wife and was told that she was not shopping wisely enough, while Peter was criticised for sleeping in on his day off (the curtains had been observed to be drawn at 9.30am). The car was too shabby, the house too untidy, the family inhospitable. And so it went on. Peter and Mary began to understand why the previous pastor and family had left after just two years. The elders had said that he had been found to be unsuitable and a little lazy, but Peter and Mary came to realise that their lives were under constant scrutiny from influential people in the church who required certain standards to be met. Peter and his family needed to get out, and fast.

Sadly this is not a far-fetched story, but is in fact an amalgam of true events. One of the dynamics facing families in the public arena is that they are on show and can feel like fish in a tank with the Church and the world staring in at them. There is a price to be paid by a 'ministering family' and it is vital that correct boundaries be put in place to enable such families to have a reasonable life.

This chapter is of particular importance to the married person but the single person should benefit from it as well. You may be married now or you may approach married life later. You may remain single but one thing is sure: if you are going to be involved in ministry within the Church you will almost certainly be involved with others who are married.

You may also have colleagues who are in ministry and are married. So then, whether or not you are married, proceed with good heart through all that follows, thinking, feeling and learning.

In this chapter you will consider a process of examination to help you to grow in your understanding of the stresses of ministry life.

1. You will focus attention on ministry and family in order to discover the kind of stressors that may be experienced here.
2. You will develop your ability to analyse 'stress factors' experienced in the ministry.
3. You will continue to develop 'awareness' skills that will help you in other areas of your life.

Some of the material in this chapter will make use of the term 'crisis'. But this is not used to denote a problem that exists, so much as to point to an acknowledgeable dynamic. This motif acts as a 'focus puller'. This process begins immediately as we begin to look at marriage and continues as we lay different veneers of experience over the marriage.

Marriage

Leaving and cleaving

Consider the following passages:

> The man said, 'This is now bone of my bones and flesh of my flesh; she shall be called "woman", for she was taken out of man.' For this reason a man will leave his father and mother and be united to his wife, and they will become one flesh. (Gen. 2:23–24)

> 'Haven't you read,' he replied, 'that at the beginning the Creator "made them male and female", and said, "For this reason a man will leave his father and mother and be united to his wife, and the two will become one flesh"? So they are no longer two, but one. Therefore what God has joined together, let man not separate.' (Matt. 19:4–6)

> 'For this reason a man will leave his father and mother and be united to his wife, and the two will become one flesh.' This is a profound mystery – but I am talking about Christ and the church. However, each one of you also must love his wife as he loves himself, and the wife must respect her husband. (Eph. 5:31–33)

The Bible indicates that marriage is a normal expression of life. It doesn't suggest that singleness is not normal, but encourages the 'leaving and cleaving' approach to life. This is not the place to expound a full theology of marriage, but marriage is a normal state of life and biblically encouraged as such.

Marriage involves a change of life from being single to being married, from one lifestyle to another. It may mean leaving the family home to set up your own. This is not true for all cultures but is particularly true in the West. It does mean leaving the earlier state and entering into a new relationship that involves bonding at a very deep level, underlined by an active, loving, sexual experience that helps to cement the relationship. 'Leaving and cleaving' means to move away from your earlier position as a son or daughter in the family home, and towards your partner, relating at a deep level, uniquely, with this one human being, so establishing a new unit. The cleaving part is often more easily coped with than the leaving. You may have spent a lifetime in a home with a regime or behavioural code to follow, providing you with a sense of stability and security, but suddenly it is down to you and your partner to establish a new life together.

Becoming one

The Bible says that a man and a woman, as a marriage partnership, become as 'one flesh'. It implies that this relationship requires something of a paradigm shift from one state or identity to another, from being a single person thinking and living within the community, to a new lifestyle and approach. You are now a married person, no longer living as the centre of your own life, but sharing life at the most intimate levels with another person, as if one flesh.

This shift involves three obvious crises or points of tension:

1. A person will need to cope with their 'new identity'. *Crisis: Who am I?*
2. A person will need to cope with living closely with another human being who is going through an identity shift. *Crisis: Who are we?*
3. The couple are now living a new lifestyle, with new identities. *Crisis: How do we now live?*

When a single person marries, changes take place at several levels for the individuals concerned. These changes have been considered as crises that occur in their lives.

Family

In this section we are adding to the scene the 'veneer' of children. A married couple have already gone through a number of changes, but now face more change as they become a family.

Marriage is the joining together of two human beings as one. The suggestion made above is that this relationship involves a number of new dynamics being experienced by those involved, but when children are included, whereas obvious and fabled changes such as sleepless nights and dirty nappies are made, there is far more taking place.

Case study

Jeremy and Sally had been married for eight years before their first child, Alice, came along. They had enjoyed each other's company and had a good marriage. They laughed, cried, argued and smiled together – the normal flow of a relationship. They hadn't exactly tried hard for a child but had been hoping, for the previous two years, that they would be 'blessed' with a baby. Sally had begun to worry that something was wrong, but all this melted away when Dr Rawlings, her GP, had announced, 'Congratulations, you are seven weeks pregnant.'

Much excitement followed, along with a flurry of preparation. Jeremy was an architect with a busy local firm, but found early on that he now needed to spend more time at home, decorating the newly furnished baby's nursery. They had decided that early in their baby's life she would have her own cot in the nursery so that their married life would not be taken over. Jeremy and Sally were not quite sure whose idea this was but it seemed to be a good one.

They made great plans together and very much looked forward to their new arrival. Jeremy had sensed a kind of butterfly feeling in his stomach whenever he and Sally talked about the baby and he put this down to anxiety over the birth to come.

The great day arrived and Alice was a healthy baby girl of seven pounds and six ounces. The delivery had gone well and Sally and Jeremy gazed down lovingly at the sleeping, crinkle-skinned baby that was their new daughter Alice.

After a few days they were able to take Alice home to her new room in her new home. They were, at last, a family.

Sally had decided long before the birth that she would breast-feed for as long as she could, to give Alice the best start in life. Jeremy had read the books and seen the documentaries and totally agreed with Sally. He had enjoyed the early weeks of this new experience but before long began to feel that Alice had all of Sally's attention now and he had none. He hated himself for what he felt, but it could be described only as jealousy for his wife's attention.

Jeremy had been unable to cope with this and before long was mentioning it to Sally, mostly in the form of a complaint. Sally took it badly and clung more to her identity as a mother with a needy child. The months went by and Sally and Jeremy became like strangers living under the same roof. Alice was rarely put in her room and Sally had moved the cot into their own bedroom, 'Just in case she needs me.' Sally and Jeremy were not resuming their formerly active and enjoyable sexual relationship and grew further and further apart.

As time passed the couple needed to go for counselling and were able to work through the problems they had encountered. They had other children and these tensions did not return in such a destructive fashion.

This couple had gone through a number of tensions or crises as their relationship changed by the addition of a new family member:

1. They were no longer a couple but a threesome. *Crisis: Who are we?*
2. They were no longer simply Jeremy and Sally but Mum and Dad. *Crisis: Who am I?*
3. They no longer lived to please themselves but had an added responsibility. *Crisis: How do we function and what is our new role?*

Jeremy felt uncomfortable about his reactions to Sally and Alice, and gave himself an emotional beating for experiencing quite understandable feelings. Our feelings are sometimes like a submarine that has been submerged out of sight for a long time. When the norms of our lives are altered by unforeseen experiences the submerged feelings begin to surface and can take us by surprise.

Jeremy loved Sally and while he realised that they would be a threesome from now on, he could not know how this would make him feel. It wasn't until he experienced it that his own feelings surfaced like the sub. Suddenly the klaxon was sounding, 'Warning! Warning! You are losing your wife's attention, and life is changing for the worse.'

In truth, life was just changing. Moving from being a twosome to being a threesome is a change and does bring the kind of crises outlined above. This is quite natural and typical. Jeremy wasn't a bad and selfish man; he was simply getting in touch with his feelings. The problem was that he had not expected the situation, and no one had told him what to expect.

Awareness is a helpful tool. To have at the very least some knowledge of what to expect can alleviate many months of suffering and could even prevent the collapse of a marriage and a family.

For you this may have been a reminder of the past. Or perhaps you are in the thick of it. Or perhaps it seems like life on another planet just now. For the purposes of this book the above hasn't been written simply as a way into pastoral care but as a means of provoking thought about major life changes.

Reflection

Reflect on the first parts of this chapter. What have they made you feel? Has it sparked some memories or provoked some recognition not previously thought through?

All of the above leads us to the next section, which prepares us to consider life as we move into the curious world of the ministry.

Marriage and family plus ministry

Using the approach above (looking deeply into the changes or crises that arise when life changes take place in the marriage and family) we now look at the addition of the ministry equation to the lives of husband, wife and children. This addition leads to a new series of crises experienced by the family.

The addition of the ministry may come to you and your family in various ways. Many now enter the ministry with marriages and families, and attitudes to marriage, family and the ministry have changed through the long history of the Church. What follows will simply assume that the minister is married, has a family and has just entered the ministry. I will mostly adopt the male minister model not out of prejudice or preference but simply from observing that more men currently work as full-time ministers throughout the denominations.

Crisis: Who am I now that the family has adopted a new identity?

Perhaps one of the first crises to be experienced revolves around the question 'Who has been called to the ministry?' Sometimes an unspoken dynamic that has not been thought through so much as taken for granted is that all the family are called to the ministry. Each reader will probably have a differing viewpoint on this, and I want to stimulate your thinking here. What do you believe about your family, and do you communicate your belief here or just stand aside? Each family member may have a different idea about this, with a set of expectations of their own and a set of expectations from other family members (which is probably normal in all families). Family members will also feel that the church places on them a set of expectations that have been either communicated or implied.

The family may feel tension through the need to fulfil these expectations for each other and for the church. The complexity of this matrix of expectation is such that no minister's family will ever succeed in fulfilling all that is expected. If the expectations are not discussed openly within the family and rationalised, allowing the individuals to be who they are, then the family will experience huge stresses and strains in their relationships. Sadly this is often the case.

Crisis: Am I so different from others?

The crisis outlined above has often developed to the point that the children of ministers have rebelled against their parents, against God and against the Church. They have felt pressured over several years to perform and can no longer face life within the Church. Just as soon as they are able to make the break they often do. They feel that they are expected to behave better than any other children in church because they are the minister's children. They feel that their parents put undue pressure on them to perform in the public eye and that to fail to do so is not only to disappoint their parents but to let the ministry down.

They are frequently aligned with the ministry, when inside they feel strongly that they are ordinary people and no different from others. These children deeply wish to be left alone to live life normally. This situation is so common that it has been given a title: 'PK syndrome' (PK = pastors' kids). They have listened to many conversations about different events and different church members over the family meal table, as their parents processed their stresses in discussion in front of them. They are really not sure what to think about Christians. Their once high opinion has been shattered. Some of these children never return to the Church and many develop a marked cynicism about the hypocrisy of Christians.

Crisis: How do we live life while being closely observed?

Another crisis that the ministry family may face has been described as 'life in a goldfish bowl'. This is descriptive of the nature of this public life. The nature of the ministering role involves being seen as having a higher profile than the average church member. Many ministers feel that they are public property and that the whole church sees everything they do. Some church members are so interested or fascinated by the minister and their family that they will engage in bizarre behaviour, as mentioned in the opening of this chapter. One minister and his wife made sure that, before they went to bed at night, they closed all the curtains at the front of the house. They didn't want anyone to know of their movements because they felt that they were constantly observed.

One wise and humorous minister's wife, on newly arriving at a church, made sure after a few days that she invited all the ladies of the church to an 'open house'. She felt that many people were so curious about the inside of the 'minister's house' that it was easier to get it all over with in one go than to go through years of prying.

Heavy pressures are experienced by those in any form of public life who constantly live in the public eye. An additional pressure for the ministering family is that together with the public gaze they face public scrutiny about the nature of their lives. They often feel that a 'jury' sits in judgment of every move they may make. They also feel that this 'jury' has no unity of thought and so they find it impossible to succeed. Constant feelings of failure may accompany the minister and their family.

Crisis: What is my role?

Ministers' spouses find a set of unique tensions in their role. It is possible for a minister's wife to feel pressurised to lead the women's fellowship, be the inspiration for the Women's World Day of Prayer, visit the members of the church that her husband cannot get around to, be the perfect hostess, counsellor and confidante, be the unpaid secretary and personal assistant to her husband, be the mother of her children, setting a shining example to other mothers, and be the sexy lover that her husband desires her to be! Many wives of serving ministers are overwhelmed with the tasks seemingly set for them and yet may experience ambiguity when trying to work out their own role. Typically a minister's wife is aware of expectations never really fitted into any kind of job description, and is often treated as if she is a co-church leader, but made to feel that she is not

– to be in the know about so much without the freedom or the platform to express her views. Role confusion is thus frequently in evidence in the life of a minister's spouse.

Crisis: Am I completely alone?

The minister's wife may feel very alone because of the above. She may feel that there is no other person like her in the church (she may be right) and that she is not understood even by her husband. She may find it very difficult to make any relationships of significance. She may feel that there is literally no one to whom she can turn. If she shares her feelings with a church member she feels that she may be betraying her husband. If she talks to her non-churched neighbour, she feels that she is letting the church down. As the result of all of this she experiences a sense of failure before God and cannot easily turn to him either. Obviously not all of the wives/husbands of ministers feel exactly like this, but many can associate closely with it.

Crisis: Am I really lovable?

The minister's spouse may feel like the proverbial 'golf widow'. Typically a couple may share a sense of call along with a sense of urgency to see people come to Christianity and for the church to grow. They may throw themselves into the work together with gusto but after a while they realise that the minister is out of the house and away from the family relationships for a considerable amount of time. This seems fine at first. It fits the 'vision'. However, relationships have deep needs for fulfilment, and fulfilment needs some form of contact and intimacy: a husband to a wife, a mother to a son, a father to a daughter, etc.

Relationships need to be fed by intimacy or they suffer seriously. Distance can lead to the death of a relationship. Lack of intimacy can lead to the breakdown of parent–child relationships and the breakdown of marriage and family.

Crisis: When is my work completed?

In keeping with the above thoughts, the problem of time exists for ministering families. Most ministers are working in a role that is self-monitoring and self-motivating. As we have seen earlier, ministers feel watched and so have three huge forces affecting their use of time:

1. *God* sees me and I want to be zealous in my work for Him.
2. *The church* sees me and I want to do a good job for them and to be seen to be doing so.
3. *I* want to do a good job for me. I want to work well and hard and give a good account of myself.

The result of these forces is that many ministers work very long hours. Most work a six- to seven-day week, with each day consisting of ten to twelve hours. That is a sixty- to eighty-four-hour week. Many ministers still take telephone calls and visitors over and above these working hours. There is a thin dividing line between work and leisure for ministers and this pattern of work is a great pressure on them and their families.

Our research, in addressing the stresses of ministry life, when considering ministers' family relationships, discovered that 31 per cent of those responding to the interviews felt that their family suffered from the fact that they had insufficient time together.

Crisis: Where do we belong?

The role of church minister often involves having to move house frequently, which uproots the family, cuts off the natural flow of relationships and removes the familiar, as the family has to settle into a new house and a new area, meet a new community of people, and establish new schools, doctors, dentists, etc. Moving house has been described as one of the higher stressors for any person or family and this can happen repeatedly during the career of a minister. It becomes difficult for the family to feel at home or put down roots anywhere. They often live in tied accommodation and this makes them feel that they are temporary residents and simply passing through. They are unsure about making lasting relationships for fear that any real investment in these will be a means of future pain. This experience can lead to a feeling of isolation for each family member, and they may feel extremely different from anyone else in the church.

Crisis: What are we worth to God and His people?

Finances are another source of stress in ministry life. Many ministering families are asked to live in areas and serve people with significantly higher incomes, and yet ministers feel the pressure to live as equals, without the financial profile to match.

In the West, we live in a society that recognises worth through financial gain. Financial profile has much to do with being rewarded for your work. The more your company pays you the more valuable you feel to it. Ministers who think like this are either consciously or sub-consciously struggling with feeling as if they are not worth much or their work is not appreciated because their pay is low. This is not universally true but is the experience of many ministers. So the following is possible:

- The minister feels undervalued.
- His or her spouse is worn out by struggling to make ends meet caring for the family.
- The children resent God and the church for making them feel like the poor kids on the block. They have suffered pain at the hands of other church children and children at school.

Of course this doesn't happen to every minister's family, but it is common. Many ministers feel poorly paid and their spouses can carry great pain as a result.

Crisis: Are we living a lie?

The spiritual life of ministers and their family suffers from the kind of crises outlined here. This, coupled with the element of spiritual pressure experienced by a family, makes it difficult for each family member to sustain a healthy spiritual life, which becomes a crisis for the minister. He sees the family drifting spiritually, begins to worry, and feels guilty that the family is not riding the proverbial crest of the spiritual wave.

- The minister feels that the family should set spiritual examples, even though no other family in the church experiences the crises in quite the same way that the minister's does.
- The children may blame God for their life experience.
- The spouse feels that they are letting the side down spiritually.

This chapter gives the appearance that a ministry role is filled with negativity and implies that nothing good can be found in such a role. Although many ministers and their families are both healthy and happy in their life and work, the potential for a negative experience does exist, and this kind of reflection may help you and others to enjoy a positive experience of ministry.

7. Sexuality and the Ministry

As this is a huge subject, this chapter can deal only with certain aspects without attempting to be a book in itself. I will focus on heterosexuality, and the chapter will be restricted to alerting the reader to the sexual dynamics that can affect the life and work of those in the ministry. It is offered as a means of reflection on what is a difficult subject and to provide material to help readers to think through their sexual self and how the ministry may be impacted by it.

Reflect on the information given and the theories propounded. Take note of the warnings here. You may consider yourself beyond any problems in this area, but read on; sex is a hugely significant part of human life that enormously impacts our emotional and spiritual lives.

Sexuality and you

Humanity and sexuality

Dr Louis McBurney, in his book *Counselling Christian Workers*,[1] propounds the theory of the 'three sexes': man, woman and the Christian minister, who is probably neuter. Incredibly, many seem to forget that Christian ministers are human beings with the same range of human emotions and needs as anyone else, although they are often regarded as another life form. McBurney suggests that this viewpoint has developed from two roots: historical ecclesiology and cultural stereotyping. From the historical perspective McBurney suggests that many Christians find it hard even to consider that their minister may have an active sex life. We probably don't want to over-encourage our church members to dwell on this, but ministers are often considered to be above or beyond such things since they spend 'so much time' with God. It sounds far too simplistic to be true but there really is truth in it. For many centuries ministers or priests were required to be celibate and this is still required in the Roman Catholic Church. In the eyes of the people, ministers were considered neuter or non-sexual.

The relationship between spirituality and sexuality is still a problem for many Christians who feel a measure of guilt surrounding their sexual lives. It's as if sex belongs to the world of sin and, for the Christian, sin and spirituality do not appear to mix, or at least not well! Something of this continues today and, while most Protestant groups would not forbid their ministers or priests to marry, the myth of 'non-sexual clergy' lingers on. So for some, sex and the man or woman of God seem worlds apart. Rarely do theological colleges include thinking or teaching about sex and the spiritual life of the clergy, other than from a general standpoint of Scripture and morality. Few Christian ministers enjoy the freedom to discuss their sexuality openly with their colleagues and even fewer would ever discuss such things with members of their own congregation.

From the cultural stereotyping perspective, McBurney draws a comparison between the media image of masculinity depicted as the muscle-bound, hard-talking hard-living tough guy and the image of the 'man of the cloth'. A minister I spoke to recently admitted to feelings of anger whenever he saw a clergyman depicted on television or in films. For him there seemed to be a deliberate distancing of type between average men and male clergy. The clergy seemed always to be physically and emotionally weak people who avoided the issues of real life. McBurney, who has used his skills and professionalism with many Christian ministers and their spouses, suggests that male clergy often feel excluded from the world of men and attempt to compensate for this with behaviour that may lead them into dangerous practices that cause suspicion.

Superhumanity

When ministers work for an extended period with the expectation that they are superhuman, they can begin to believe it. It is quite possible that many Christian ministers believe themselves to be safe with regard to their sexuality. They consider that their calling and ordination has given them a cloak of steel like that of the fictional character Batman, who uses his cloak to ward off attack. This belief is probably an ingredient for a number of such ministers falling into sexual sin. Like blindness that causes a person to stumble and fall, Christian ministers stumble into their humanity. They need to be more aware of their vulnerability and sexuality and to realise that their work will bring them into situations that may be threatening.

Normal temptations

Western society has become highly sexualised, with sex being used like a huge, powerful magnet to sell anything from washing powder to cars. Exposure to such imagery and overt sexuality on a regular basis has the effect of lowering thresholds and changing social sexual boundaries. This effect touches most human beings and the Christian minister is no different. The temptation to lower their personal standards is great and increases as society embraces a casual attitude towards the place of sex in human relationships. Christian ministers are tempted, like anyone else, and need to recognise this for themselves.

Sexual development

There are a number of changes that take place in the life of any person as he or she develops sexually. These stages are common to all human beings; for example, the 'early stage', when children become fascinated with sexuality and seek to compare their bodies with those of the opposite sex. 'You show me yours and I'll show you mine' is a normal stage of sexual development. As children move into puberty they will often explore further by experiencing orgasm through self-stimulation, which is quite normal and highly common as human beings relate to their sexuality. This is not the place to discuss fully every stage of sexual development, but suffice to say that we all develop sexually.

Our development may be positively or negatively affected at any point along this developmental continuum, as sexuality is a powerful and ever-present force within each of us. It may cause us to be overconfident or shy towards the opposite sex. It has the power to generate a private world with secret difficulties that we are reluctant to talk about with anyone. Our sexual development may even become a gaoler, as it imprisons our emotions and binds us to difficulties. The interventions in our sexual development may cause us to develop problems that stay with us into our adult lives and sometimes for the rest of our lives.

Case study

Reg was just thirteen years old. He was at that stage where his dreams were sexy, and he was embarrassed by what he considered to be his bad thoughts. He had been brought up to believe that sex was not to be discussed, as it was a dirty subject. He couldn't stop his dreams but his sense of shame was strong. One day, while waiting for a bus, some of his older brother's friends pulled up in a van and offered to give him a lift to school.

Reg accepted the lift and had been in the van for just a minute or two when one of the other occupants said, 'Here, take a look at these', and handed him a wad of photographs. The pictures were of naked men and women engaged in various sexual acts. They were explicit in the extreme. This incident was to stay with Reg for many years to come and to be a constant source of agony.

Reg felt a shockwave move through his body. He had never seen anything like this before and was literally stunned into silence as if he had been hit with a blunt instrument. All that day Reg could still see in his mind's eye those powerful sexual images. Days and weeks went by but he was still plagued by the images. He engaged in masturbation regularly until it became a binding habit that he found difficult to control. His sense of shame increased and he began to believe that he must be the only person in the world to have such a dirty mind. He developed a low sense of self-esteem that was to be a long-term problem.

Years on, Reg became a Christian and eventually entered the ministry. He had seen his conversion as a victory over his former life but was still dogged by images. As he grew he had struggled with the desire to look at more explicit photographs and was often tempted to buy pornographic magazines. After a time in the ministry, Reg began a double life. It seemed the only thing he could do. He had decided in a moment of extreme stress to keep his sexual problems secret and separate. He would be a good Christian minister but engage in this private life. He began driving out of town where no one would know him so that he could buy his magazines. He suffered greatly from these pressures until he could face it no longer. Coming close to emotional collapse he confessed his story to a sensitive counsellor. His ministry had been a struggle up till then: he was afraid of women because of his sexual fantasies, and of men because he was sure they could tell what a 'dirty-minded' man he was. Reg had been wounded in his sexual development and was only able to gain his freedom as he was helped to put the pieces together and begin to understand himself.

Reg eventually married and found sexual fulfilment in the loving intimacy of marriage – he had never before considered marriage because he felt so unworthy. He has been able to continue in his ministry without the repeated images and temptations. He completed the development of his sexuality by growing in his self-awareness.

Christian ministers need to become aware of the stages of their sexual development and ask themselves some serious questions about any unresolved sexual issues.

Reflection

This is deeply personal and may be difficult for you, possibly even painful. Reflect on your sexual journey so far. Are you aware of any problems or stresses with regard to your sexual development? Do problems relating to this exist for you now?

I encourage any Christian leaders struggling with sexual issues to take a period of professional counselling. This is not to suggest that there is anything wrong with them or that they are particularly needy, but that the stresses of the ministry have a tendency to compound sexual and emotional problems. Actively committing to the resolving of personal issues is a mature and peace-bringing approach to life. Ideally the selection/training process for the ministry should include discreet opportunities for candidates to discuss and work through any issues of an emotional or sexual nature with a counsellor, before they begin to work full-time in the ministry.

Theory on sexual difficulties

Sexual difficulties can cause human beings to struggle for many years, and sometimes, if left, for a lifetime. They can cause an individual to enter into a double life, one lived out publicly, and the other a dark and private world of fear, guilt and pain. Sometimes this private world is so private that no other human being, not even a spouse, will get to know about it. This makes for a lonely and difficult life. The human energy required to live with painful secrets is immense and sufferers are often tired and worn out from living this existence. Letting light into the darkness brings great healing, and facing the issues with sensitive help can break the chains of years of private hell.

Although there are many theories on sexual difficulties I would like to highlight two here. Both have to do with the area of self-awareness mentioned earlier in this book and heavily underline that thinking. One is the theory of 'sexual addiction', and the other postulates that some sexual problems are due to 'personal wounding', where ministers bring their own needs for healing into the ministry arena. I believe that both of these views have something helpful to say and that they have an element of overlap.

Sexual addiction

This is an observable condition defined by Dr Harry W. Schaumburg[2] as a condition or state of mind that is connected with the fear of intimacy. This theory suggests that a person may adopt a behavioural pattern that allows them to look for sexual gratification outside an intimate personal relationship, not simply as the answer to a moment's need, but as a life pattern that moves people further away from what they really desire; that is, an intimate, personal, loving relationship. The more they pursue this false intimacy, the less there will be a chance of real intimacy.

This wide concept encompasses a continuum. At one end of the spectrum is the person who, at the end of a day at the office, prefers to look at a glossy magazine and masturbate rather than go to bed with his wife and make love. Such a person is focused on personal gratification and does not want to deal with the needs of his partner with the foreplay saga and the loving build-up to intercourse. At the other extreme is the person who pays to have sex with a prostitute a few times a month and has no other sexual relationship with anyone. The rush of adrenaline and the physical experience of orgasm becomes addictive in and of itself, without the connection to a caring relationship. This can result in a person preying on others, seeing them as objects of gratification rather than people. Once this mindset is entered into, the caring nature of the relationship is lost. It is possible that there never was a caring relationship. For some, this problem is the cause of loneliness since they find it difficult to relate to others.

The continuum is lengthy and there are many descriptions of different levels of sexual addiction. Preying on human beings as a source of sexual gratification is a common trait in the Western world, and this trait can even exist in the Christian ministry. There have been occasions when ministers have manipulated circumstances, such as the time and place of appointments, to coincide with the maximum possibility for sexual misconduct. Or they have literally selected members of the opposite sex and have mounted campaigns with the hope of conquest, usually resulting in sexual intimacy with a highly vulnerable person.

In the late twentieth century there were a number of widely reported stories in which high-profile Christian ministers resorted to inappropriate sexual practices. Most engaged in sexual acts with prostitutes in the vain hope that they were doing so away from the public eye. It seems incredible that such ministers could continue to minister while living this double life. Such people have undoubtedly reached a point in their emotional lives where sex is disconnected from an emotional and meaningful relationship with the one they love and has become a means of feeding a craving with a quick fix. This form of sexual practice can never be fulfilling. The individual concerned is in desperate need of a deep and satisfying relationship but is kept from it by the quick-fix mentality. These issues negatively impact the spiritual and emotional life of the sex addict and have disastrous effects upon their victims. Relationships take time and emotional energy to maintain. If, for whatever reason, people are not taking the time to invest in their marriage, then the quick fix can be an enormous temptation.

Sexual addiction is a powerful driving force that takes huge risks with family, friends and profession. As with alcoholism and drug addiction, life is damaged to fulfil the desire. Those who suffer from this form of addiction often have huge problems with guilt and find it difficult to live at peace in their work or home lives. The impact of this kind of problem on a marriage is considerable. Typically, a couple find themselves arguing about the quality and quantity of love and sex within their marriage and they are often unable to work out their differences, which sometimes results in a drawing apart. For the sex addict, the appetite for sexual gratification can reach such proportions that concentration on anything else can be difficult and normal life function can be severely disturbed.

I have pointed out that there is a continuum of sexual addiction and that it really begins for some when the pursuit of personal sexual gratification is separated from deep loving relationships. My prognosis is that the Western world, with its emphasis on regular casual sex outside the marriage relationship, continually runs the risk of creating an epidemic in this arena. I believe that sexual addiction can begin in puberty where self-exploration (normal experiments with masturbation) becomes a habitual form of self-comfort. Like many other forms of addiction, the need to comfort our pain can lead to the misuse of reasonable practices until they take a grip on our lives and begin to have power over us and, in this instance, become our sexual motif.

Personal wounding

This theory assumes that all men and women have a degree of emotional wounding and that the need for healing from our wounds can become a dominant process in our lives. The thought here is that our wounds, especially in men, will often affect us at the level of our sexuality. Men will look to sex for healing and/or comfort, the comfort found in the intimacy of sexuality.

My own observations lead me to believe that many ministering persons (perhaps most) who have fallen into sexual sin with others have done so because of their wounding. Wounding is seen here as the hurting or disturbing of inner peace and security, leading to feelings of insecurity and the heightened need for emotional comfort. Personal discoveries, as seen in the following story, can be made in the wrong places:

Case study

Tom, the pastor of a Free Church in the north of England, essentially married his mother when, as a young man of twenty-one, he met a woman with the same dominant nature as his mother. Tom's mother had dominated his father until, after fifteen years of married life, he could stand it no longer and left, for good. Tom, who was ten when this happened, blamed his father and regarded him as weak. His father never seemed to make any decisions or know what to do when things got difficult. Tom could always rely on his mother, who invariably made things better. She was constantly in control!

Later, Tom met Lucy. He was away from home and at college when they met and was feeling particularly vulnerable without his mother around. He wouldn't admit it to himself because he despised the thought of seeming like his father – a weak man. Lucy was full of energy. She knew where she was going and how to get there. They were at the Christian Union together and she would frequently encourage Tom to stand up and speak up. Tom thought that they were the ideal couple – he felt strong and safe around her. He was in love and they married at the end of their college life. Lucy encouraged Tom to enter the ministry where he would make a difference to the world and be at the cutting edge of the Christian life.

After a few years as a pastor, Tom felt that effort and failure had blunted his edge. He felt tired and alone. Lucy was a great attraction in the church; she attended everything and her views were respected, but he felt lonely and out of his depth. He went on like this, feeling quite miserable, until Kate joined the church. Kate was not a beautiful-looking woman but was friendly and pleasant to be with. She was prepared to help with any church projects but never wanted to be the leader. Eventually Kate became Tom's administrative assistant at the church office. Tom enjoyed this and grew very fond of Kate. Kate would often refer to the feelings of security she experienced around Tom and he began to feed off these new feelings. Never before had anyone felt safe with him and he had never felt more like a man than he did with Kate – only with Kate!

What followed is tragic. Tom left Lucy, the ministry and the church with the first big decision he had ever made for himself, and started a new life with Kate. Tom had been wrestling with his personal wounding without knowing it. Kate met him at a point of deep-rooted emotional need and Tom fed from it like a starving man. Tom has never returned to the ministry or the church. He had been wounded in early life by the misuse of power and aggression that had distorted his views of the true nature of relationship. He had grown to believe that he needed to have a strong mother figure around him instead of a person with whom he could enjoy a balanced and mutual relationship. He had been starved by the lack of awareness of his own resources. Sadly his self-discovery, too late, led to the end of his ministry.

Facing our wounds before tragedy strikes or before big life decisions are made is by far the best policy. In truth, few people are made aware of this need until they are attempting to handle the havoc in their lives.

Emotional need, then, can lead us into inappropriate sexual behaviour and relationships. Students need to reflect on this material to endeavour to get in touch with their own emotional dimensions. If you find this to be a problem or some difficult issues are raised for you, I recommend you seek out the help of an adviser, mentor or counsellor to help you work through this.

In a survey of clergymen reported by the Center for the Prevention of Sexual and Domestic Violence of Seattle, Washington, the number of ministers who have engaged in some form of sexual contact with a church member was 38.6 per cent, while the number who had sexual intercourse with a church member was 12.7 per cent. Of the respondents, 76.5 per cent 'know of' ministers who have had sexual intercourse with a church member who was not their spouse.

Research in the UK has shown that 29 per cent of the respondents (ministering persons from a wide range of churches and denominations) have had some sexual involvement with those in their pastoral care. These are startling figures and, if they were to be applied across the board, would indicate that almost a third of all serving church ministers have been sexually involved in some way with people in their pastoral care.

Sexuality and emotional hunger

The Bible teaches that human beings were created to be in community. We were created to be social, not solitary, beings. Experiments exposing people to long periods of solitude have shown that when the average human being is left alone for extended periods of time, he or she suffers physically and psychologically. Withdrawal from others could be said to be harmful to our health. Our lives are best lived, not independently, but interdependently, since our health requires that we have meaningful relationships with those around us.

The need to love and be loved

Love, as a phenomenon, has been studied by various cultures, and has delivered a plethora of findings. The one common factor is that human beings need to be valued unconditionally, prized not so much for *what* they are as *who* they are. If a human being is deprived of being so valued (unconditional positive regard), then they begin to suffer from its withdrawal or absence. This deprivation can be actual (no one loves the person) or fantasy (a belief that they are not loved). Such a reality or belief seems to release powerful, self-destructive psychological mechanisms. Often, unhealthy levels of low self-worth are experienced and, in extreme cases, some people even resort to suicide.

Similarly, when a human being is unable to express love to another human being, for either real or imaginary reasons, that person may sink to a similar state of low self-worth. Out of love we were created, and called by this same love to give love to God and to fellow human beings.

The need for warmth and physical touch

Another facet of the human social make-up is the need for warmth as an expression of love. This is a genuine *need* that is met by marriage, family, friendship, etc. Emotional problems arise if this warmth is not expressed or received when a person is so deprived. The word 'deprived' is a good one to use here, since it indicates the seriousness of such a missing element in a person's life. Most people who are deprived of love will develop a negative personal belief system, and some will literally ache for human touch. Others may turn in on themselves with destructive anger expressed in an 'I don't need anyone else' mentality – like a self-fulfilling prophecy they bring about a greater withdrawal from other human beings, causing further suffering to themselves.

Like a mouth to feed

Human emotional need is very much like appetite. Not only can we become emotionally hungry, but we can also become starving. This emotional hunger, while not as noticeable as the need for food, is still real and develops into an emotional wound if not attended to. The hunger sometimes grows slowly without the sufferers necessarily realising that they are becoming hungry. Such need will often be hidden until it has reached starvation proportions and then the emotions will reach out to be fed. When this happens, the emotionally starving person may reach out to the wrong source for sustenance.

Case study

Jack and Jane have been married for seventeen years and Jack is a vicar. They have been in the ministry for twelve years and have a happy marriage. Neither considers that they have a problem or that they are vulnerable to marital breakdown. Sadly, in their relationship a hidden bomb is ticking towards detonation.

Jack and Jane shared a strong sense of 'call' together and determined that they would work as a couple in the ministry. True to this conviction, they have worked faithfully and are now five years into their second church. They feel confident about their work in this medium-sized church that is a little slow to change, but Jack feels somewhat held back in his hopes for the congregation. Everything seems to take so long to come about and for some time Jack has been working more evenings than planned. Jane is fortunately understanding and is committed to the church. Jack and Jane are having less time together and have discussed this, but both agree that the church's need is great. They used to spend two evenings a week with each other, but once in two weeks is now OK. They used to make love at least once a week, but now it's once a month, and this is OK. The pattern repeats, while the bomb, unseen, lies in wait to unleash its destructive forces!

What they have failed to see is that they are creating a situation where they are not serving their emotional needs; they are in fact creating emotional wounds. Jack often counsels people from the church and community. He is really quite good at it, offering warmth and sincerity to the needy. Susan was married but her husband left her for another woman. A friend told her that the local vicar is very good at helping in times of need. The appointment is made. Jack and Jane are happy that they seem to be reaching the community. Jack and Susan meet and things go well. Susan is pleased and tells Jack what a great help he is. She pats his hand and leaves, having made her next appointment. The day arrives. Jack is tired but feels a sense of responsibility. Susan opens up to him with more of her hurt; Jack reaches out with sincere compassion. He holds her as she weeps, and little by little the embrace takes on a different shape – and before they realise it, they have kissed. It could stop there, but Jack is starving emotionally and his whole system cries out. Susan's touch and her obvious need is like a magnet to Jack, like an electric shock. The bomb explodes with a wave of destruction, shattering love, life and marriage.

This is typical of the way in which many relationships begin. In this case, the relationship came to the point where Jack crossed the line. He was the mentor or carer. He was the professional, but overstepped the mark. He had the responsibility to take care of the client or counsellee, to provide a safe place; but his own needs lay in wait, ready to grasp at the next show of affection. He may have been aware of a growing interest in Susan, but couldn't admit it to himself until it was too late.

Similar circumstances have led to complex, sexually intimate relationships that result in devastation to marriage, family, church and community. Hopes and dreams are snuffed out instantly, like a gust of icy wind blowing out a candle flame.

This case study sounds like a far-fetched romantic novel, but is typical of the circumstances surrounding many of the cases where Christian ministers have crossed the line and entered into sin through sexual misconduct. Emotional hunger is a great cause for concern. When Christian ministers and others in the caring professions give of themselves without reference to their own needs or those of their families disaster can result.

Unmet emotional need will not simply dissipate, but will remain until a person has been in intimate contact (not necessarily sexual contact) with another. Stressful roles such as that of a minister lead to tragedy where they fail to take this dynamic into account.

Intimacy, sensuality and spirituality

Christianity offers itself as a living faith, not just a belief but an experience: God is 'in the midst' of His people. As a result, much of what takes place within the public framework of the practice of the faith involves a measure of intimacy. We are urged to 'Love one another' (John 13:34) and to 'Greet one another with a holy kiss' (Rom. 16:16). God's involvement with us draws us to a deeper level of involvement with each other. This represents an involved and loving community relationship that can be maintained only by people who also take care of their emotional and relational needs.

Intimacy

Many local churches would describe themselves as a family, which implies a level of relationship that goes deeper than most casual acquaintances. Christians are urged to get directly involved with each other's lives (Heb. 3:13). We effectively go through the process of lowering the interpersonal barriers between each other and with God.

We encourage openness that is a form of intimacy, where we will share our lives and sometimes our most personal thoughts and feelings in the name of family, with the understanding that church is a safe place, perhaps the only safe place, where this can be done. Tears and laughter, expressions from deep within, are features found in many of our churches. In some settings a ministry time will be offered where people may literally abandon themselves by falling into the arms of others, such is their sense of security. We need to realise the nature of our faith and understand that it can bring people together innocently in a warm, sincere, friendly environment that offers healthy levels of loving care, although this is not without a price tag. We must remain aware of the lowered interpersonal barriers and the heightened need to keep church safe. The intimacy of the church family can be carried over into the counselling room where it is not so public or so safe, with disastrous results.

Case study

In the first year of John's career as a minister, a young couple joined the church. As this was the couple's first time as members of a church, it seemed to John that he and his wife needed to spend time nurturing these two people who had arrived at the church with a number of personal needs.

They looked to John and his wife for help with their troubled marriage and confused lifestyle. The ministering couple spent a great deal of time with the newcomers and became close friends with them. John had a need to be needed that he had not seen or understood before, and began feeding on this mentor–protégé relationship.[3] He greatly looked forward to these times of meeting together and believed that God had brought along the 'first-fruit' of what was to be a blessed ministry.

The couple would take up as much time, and more, as John and his wife were prepared to give. John would often go to the house when the husband was at work and do church errands with the woman while his own wife was busy with their children. He saw no harm in this, as he genuinely meant only good for them. But he had not noticed that he was pulling away from the needs of others in the church, and indeed from his own wife and family, and was spending more and more time in the company of a charming but needy woman, who told John how great life had become since he had come into their lives. This is precisely what he wanted to hear. John was not aware of his attraction to this woman, as he was not in touch with his own needs or areas of vulnerability.

One day, after they had returned from a shopping trip for the church, John was saying goodbye at the door when, in a brotherly embrace, he kissed the woman passionately. He hadn't expected it and hadn't realised that his own needs were so raw at that time. This situation ended quickly, though, and John was able to remain as the minister (particularly since most of the church didn't find out about it), having been frightened into a course of action by the events. He told his wife and the woman's husband about what had happened. John's relationship with this woman began innocently, was ill-advised, and became intimate. He had allowed himself to cross the line and brought heartache to all concerned.

Sensuality

In the last subsection, the intimate nature of Christianity was discussed. Similarly, the practices of the Christian Church contain aspects designed to affect the worshipper. They are offered as aids to worship, elements that express to the worshipper and to God the intimate nature of the relationship with Him. Christian worship, then, often includes profoundly moving aspects. Many people report that at times in their worship they reach a place of spiritual ecstasy not found elsewhere. Often worshippers' senses are heightened as they reach out with all of their being to their God, their ever-present Father. This involves the engaging of our senses in the presence of others. Expressions of love may flow freely among such a group of worshippers who may join hands or embrace as they give themselves to the moment. This is undoubtedly an innocent form of worship, but it too carries a price tag. Christian worship is frequently sensual and as such involves the lowering of interpersonal boundaries. Sometimes the boundary between worship and the rest of life can become blurred and that feeling of intimacy is carried over, making sexual misconduct more easily entered into.

I am not suggesting that following a period of worship people are more prone to sin, but that the lowering of boundaries and the increase of familiarity within a church makes it more possible at other times for boundaries to become blurred. Interpersonal boundaries can be both a blessing and a curse.

In this section, I am not suggesting that intimacy and sensuality are negative aspects of the spiritual life, but that we must acknowledge that these aspects exist. Moreover, they bring us into contact with fellow human beings to such a degree that without vigilance we may cross the boundaries into inappropriate behaviour, as many unwary Christian ministers have done.

> Almost 80 percent of the women I spoke with had an incident to recount about having been approached sexually by a man who was her doctor, therapist, pastor, lawyer or teacher. In about half of the cases, an actual sexual relationship took place, with disastrous results.[4]

Reflection

Have you ever, in your ministry, found yourself struggling emotionally with the close proximity of another person? How did you deal with the situation?

Boundaries

During the course of this section of the chapter I have repeatedly referred to 'the boundary'. This line delineating the 'forbidden zone', as it has been called, is the point at which the therapeutic or spiritual aspect of caring has given way to a level of intimacy that includes inappropriate behaviour. Wherever there are caring professions, there are growing numbers of people crossing the line.

Defining a boundary

In the USA the Center for the Prevention of Sexual and Domestic Violence describes relationships like this:

> 'Professional relationship': a relationship whose purpose is to meet the congregant/client's need for professional (ministerial) assistance or service.
> 'Personal relationship': a relationship whose purpose is to meet the personal needs of the people involved.[5]

There is an essential difference in role and relationship between these two types. The Center would maintain that a dual relationship – that is, one that attempts to be both of the above – is a *danger zone*.

Essentially, then, the Center recommends that we, as 'carers', recognise the difference between these types of relationship and engage in the *professional relationship* alone with clients. Clients would be seen as those whom we serve as Christian ministers. Effectively the Center draws up for us a definition of a 'boundary'. Such a boundary would create difficulty for those in ministry who see themselves as having both personal and professional relationships with church members, which gives an almost clinical and unnatural feel to such relationships within the church. This is perhaps more easily achieved by doctors and counsellors, but helpfully points out for us the need for standards of professional safety to be maintained within the church. Perhaps we need to ask ourselves seriously how we can differentiate between appropriate and inappropriate behaviour.

Whether or not we agree with this definition of the boundary, few of us would argue that sexual relationships within the mentor–protégé relationship are wrong. There exists a power imbalance when a man or woman considers the mentor as having some experience or skill that will be used for the good of the person being counselled. People being counselled will often yield parts of their personal life to their counsellor/carer/minister, and will trust their counsellor/carer/minister to know how to keep the boundaries. They will expect this power imbalance, into which they freely enter, to be used for their own good. The intimacy of Christian relationships, discussed earlier, is dependent on there being a safe and trusted place.

While it may appear that expressions such as 'inappropriate' and 'sexual misconduct' are to some extent ethical judgments and may imply particular views, there exists between minister and church member an implicit agreement of trust. In this, the power ratio in the relationship is heavily weighted in the direction of the minister. The minister will often be perceived as both trustworthy and focused on the needs of the church member, who trusts the minister to provide a professional and safe caring environment. Rutter has this to say:

> The power differential begins when a person's specific need looks for help from someone more knowledgeable, trained, or competent. Once the relationship begins, the power to impose the will grows immeasurably, because the more powerful person can threaten to abandon the relationship. Trust refers to the assumption by the person with less power that the person with greater power will act in their best interest. This assumption has its inner source in the model of the parent–child relationship. The tendency to trust is reinforced, even invited, by the professions themselves, which have codes of ethics asserting that the interest of the patient, client, student, congregant, or protégé must be held uppermost, and that sexual contact is not permissible.[6]

When a situation is set up for a person to receive personal care from another, it is quite possible that either person's emotional wounding may affect the outcome. From whatever source, either person (perhaps both) may be wounded, and may comfort the hurt in the arms of a vulnerable person. Again, the vulnerable person may be either or, as is often the case, both. Mistaking their fantasy of their carer or of the one they are caring for as reality, either party may cross the line. Thus crossing the line may be at the initiative of either the mentor or the protégé.

People in need may 'fall in love' with their mentors. They may reach out with transference of their needs to the carer. Carers must be aware of the boundaries and not allow any of their own needs to enter the professional relationship.

> Clearly, the men who are the healers in forbidden-zone relationships often have as much need to be healed through them as do the protégés. When a man is feeling his wound and a woman's sexuality becomes available to him through the protected, secret conditions of the forbidden zone, the tendency to avail himself of this opportunity can become irresistible.[7]

With regard to crossing the line, the Center draws a parallel with incestuous relationships. Below is an outline of some of the dynamics found in incestuous cases and also in cases of sexual misconduct by carers:

- It takes place in the context of intimacy.
- It is committed by an authority figure.
- The victim is vulnerable.
- The offender is protected.
- If the victim discloses information, it is often disbelieved.
- Typically the victim is blamed and the offender excused.
- The victim is silenced by pressure.
- The victim is made responsible for maintaining secrecy.

It seems strange to think of members of the caring profession being likened to those who have had incestuous sexual relationships, until you consider the similarities of the details. Such a view would cause us to have great sympathy for the victim and to look to ways to bring about a helpful healing process. I agree with this and hold to the view that restitution should be made to victims of such abuse. However, I also consider that in a sense the abuser or the carer who has crossed the boundary has needs that also require a healing focus. He has confused the circumstances, and his own inner needs have come to the fore.[8]

In some cases a carer has been, in a sense, victimised by the sexual agenda of the client. Some people have deliberately gone out of their way to find sexual and emotional comfort by sexually approaching their carer. While having some sympathy for the carer in these circumstances, I take the view that the carer, as the professional, has the sole responsibility to prevent boundary violations.

> Whether they had never learned to recognise boundaries or whether they blocked out their awareness under psychological pressure, more than half the women I interviewed were not aware that it was a specific ethical violation for a man who was their therapist, pastor, teacher, or lawyer to have sex with them. Such women are at a terrible disadvantage if they have been denied this fundamental reality. The ethical codes of most male dominated professions clearly state that sexual relationships with people under their care are wrong.[9]

A greater focus on these needs, and a healthier emphasis on the requirement for professional carers to receive regular counsel throughout their working lives, would, I believe, help to prevent some of these appalling and painful situations from occurring.

Statistics have shown that the victims of professional abuse often take a long time to get over their negative experiences and have been spiritually, emotionally, psychologically, and sometimes physically, harmed by their encounters.

Reflection

What has this chapter made you feel? Are you more aware of the possible dangers here?

Students who take the course upon which this book is based engage in a task to help them come to terms with how they view an appropriate boundary. You could reflect upon the following and consider your own views. Which of these activities, in the light of this chapter, do you now consider as appropriate behaviour for a minister? (Change 'she' to 'he' as appropriate.)

- I held her hand.
- I hugged her.
- I sat a few feet away and never left my chair.
- She said that she felt ugly; I said that she was good-looking.
- She said, 'No one will find me attractive.' I said, 'Well, I do.'
- We used to meet in the park.
- I always counsel alone.
- I complimented her dress sense.
- She bought me little gifts, just to say thank you.
- I felt that she was special.
- I never counsel the opposite sex alone.
- I shared my life and my needs with her.
- My love for her is OK because I'm single.
- Emotional attachment and sexual attachment are very different.

Practical steps to boundary-setting

Setting a boundary – a line that must not be crossed in relationships where we have the responsibility as the professional carer – becomes the requirement of all caring professionals. What follows is a short list of practical (almost obvious) steps that can prove helpful in establishing boundaries:

1. *Soul search* Ask yourself how you are doing. Take a quick check of your emotional needs or hunger. Be honest with your own needs before you take on the client.[10]
2. *Attraction* Honestly ask yourself if you are attracted to your client. If you are, double your steps to safeguard the situation.
3. *Location* Ask yourself whether the place where you are to meet with your client is a 'safe place'.
4. *Policy* Consider setting a church policy that no members of the opposite sex will meet alone in the mentor–protégé relationship. This will mean female to female, male to male only. This doubling-up of carers needs careful handling with the client, and issues of confidentiality need to be addressed. Care needs to be taken also since co-mentors will be working together in a situation of considerable intimacy and the interpersonal boundaries may become distorted. If a client is struggling with homosexual issues it may be helpful also to double up as male and female with the client.
5. *Alone?* Consider working with the opposite sex only in a building

where there are others around and where others know you are working.

6. *Partners* Never break the bounds of confidentiality, but if you have a spouse share any experiences of attraction or powerful emotions regarding your client. Your relationship should be strong enough to take such frank discussions. If you keep your feelings secret you are beginning to cross the line.
7. *Reality* Never consider yourself above all of this. Remember your humanity and vulnerability.

Overcoming our sexual problems

Perhaps the first thing to say under this heading is that carers of any kind should not wait until they have experienced problems with their clients before they deal with any apparent sexual or emotional issues they may have. There is never a better time than now to focus with another on your own needs, problems, feelings, etc. In the UK, the stigma of taking 'professional help' is thankfully breaking down and people are slowly coming to realise that getting help is an act of maturity and not weakness. Many professionals are required by their organisations to take regular therapy as part of their approach to working with others. Some require, at the very least, that their professionals take monthly supervision as a system of accountability.

Christian ministers on the whole have less personal and regular accountability built into their roles than members of any other caring profession. Many ministers go through years of Christian service without giving an account of their working practices to anyone – they are trusted to get on with the job. This level of trust could be seen as a level of abandonment to a role that requires so much, so often.

Sharing the need

Let me underline here what has effectively already been said. I encourage you to have regular supervision of your work. Share your life and work with another professional who will be able to bring advice and a different perspective.

Openness

Develop a mindset of openness about your life. You do not need to relate to everyone you meet the intimate details of your life, but simply adopt a new level of honesty and openness. Remember never to keep secret those things that emotionally disturb you. Share them with someone you trust.

Counselling

Where necessary go to see a counsellor to discuss what has happened and is now happening in your life.

Spiritual director

Depending upon the nature of your working relationship with your spiritual director, this may be a 'safe place' in which to develop your openness.

Support groups

Establish a personal support group: a group of trusted people who will regularly talk with you and pray for you.

Peer groups

Form a peer group with colleagues who are in the ministry. This should be a group of trusted peers with whom you can be honest about life and ministry.

Marriage

Honesty in this relationship is essential. It is almost impossible to think that you and your spouse, having found each other attractive, will never find another person attractive. Attraction is natural and not sinful. What you do about the attraction is where the sin may lurk. Share together each other's attractions and keep them in the light. If your marriage suffers over some of the dimensions mentioned in this section, then first seek out a counsellor, and second seek out a marriage enrichment course.

Crossing the line

It is important to understand the deep-rooted causes of sexual misconduct. Few ministers set out to cross the boundary. Many have crossed it in the heat of the moment and have deeply regretted their actions. It is important that those who have crossed the line are treated as human beings and not as monsters.

Victim support

It is important that victims of sexual or emotional abuse by ministers be introduced to a same-sex counsellor/supporter very quickly. Under no circumstances should the abuser, however repentant, be allowed to offer help to the victim. A same-sex advocate who can speak for the victim needs to be appointed in order that the victim is not further abused by the system of enquiry.

Restored to role

Each denomination and organisation will have its own policy as to whether a person who has broken sexual boundaries can be restored to their position as a trusted minister. It is not possible to legislate here. I appeal to those seeking to be so restored that they ask themselves seriously whether they have faced their own inner issues and have taken appropriate therapeutic measures.

What a day it would be if the media were forced, by the weight of evidence, to declare that the Christian Church was the safest of environments for the needy to find help. Perhaps then it would be truly representative of the models of love and care that Jesus demonstrated for us in His life and teaching.

8. Ministry and the Devotional Life

There have been times when I have decided never to read books on the devotional life again. They have challenged me, scared me, accused me and have sometimes completely messed up my sleep pattern by suggesting that I should get up at some unearthly hour when the rest of the world is sleeping. In those times I invented 'sleeping in the spirit' – the ability to sleep and pray when, for all of the world, it looks as if I am asleep!

Approaching this subject may invoke one of two major feelings: joy at having the freedom to explore a subject close to your heart; terror at having to go through a chapter dealing with a subject that haunts you. It can be the one major area that brings intense feelings of guilt and failure. The title 'devotional life' suggests that we spend time 'devoted' to, communicating with and hearing from God. Within the Church there are a vast number of ways of approaching this subject.

Our research showed that when those in full-time Christian ministry were asked about their devotional lives, 61 per cent of the respondents felt that the 'devotional life' was their top priority and 39 per cent didn't. Only 9 per cent of the respondents reported that they enjoyed this activity. Some 52 per cent believed it to be the top priority but didn't enjoy it. This 52 per cent may well be living with the tension and stress of needing to fulfil a task they really don't enjoy. Like 'forced labour' they are compelled by their spirituality to consider devotions as important, but find little pleasure in the experience.

Reflection

How do you relate to your devotional life? Are you in the 9 per cent or the 52 per cent?

In this chapter we are focusing on the devotional life. The chapter is aimed at relieving some of the stresses experienced in this vital area of ministry life and promoting a healthy approach to our devotions. During the course of this you will be encouraged to think and reflect deeply on your current relationship with God. You will also be faced with some alternative thinking that may provoke a range of responses within you.

Expectations

Of God

Case study

Some clergymen were holding a discussion about the attendant 'feelings' surrounding the perceived presence of God. One said with great enthusiasm and authority that he felt a 'thickening' of the atmosphere and knew that God was present at such times. Another said that there was a profound silence that he could almost hear. He felt that the true presence of God was therefore indicated by such a silence. He found singing or music difficult to cope with in his devotional life. This viewpoint provoked an impassioned response from another who said that he always turned on the tape player with a worship cassette and felt God's closeness while surrounded by music and praise. Yet another said that he felt God's presence as a 'tingle' when he prayed. He felt that the absence of the tingle suggested the absence of God. He said that he would pray for long periods in the hope that he would experience this 'tingling' presence and that he was disappointed when God didn't seem to show up. The conversation went on through the use of candles and incense and on to the startling suggestion by one that God's presence could not be felt and that to rely on feelings was not a Christian response. The discussion drew to a sudden conclusion when one among them said that he felt that God was always present regardless of our feelings or non-feelings.

Who was right in this conversation? The answer is that they all were. As individuals we approach the approachable God in many valid ways.

If the countryside is viewed on a day trip from the city by looking through a tube, then one will certainly be disappointed by the view and fail to appreciate the wonder of the full panorama. This is also true in our approach to God and our expectations of Him in our devotional lives.

> There he went into a cave and spent the night. And the word of the LORD came to him: 'What are you doing here, Elijah?' He replied, 'I have been very zealous for the LORD God Almighty. The Israelites have rejected your covenant, broken down your altars, and put your prophets to death with the sword. I am the only one left, and now they are trying to kill me too.' The LORD said, 'Go out and stand on the mountain in the presence of the LORD, for the LORD is about to pass by.' Then a great and powerful wind tore the mountains apart and shattered the rocks before the LORD, but the LORD was not in the wind. After the wind there was an earthquake, but the LORD was not in the earthquake. After the earthquake came a fire, but the LORD was not in the fire. And after the fire came a gentle whisper. When Elijah heard it, he pulled his cloak over his face and went out and stood at the mouth of the cave. Then a voice said to him, 'What are you doing here, Elijah?' (1 Kings 19:9–13)

We may think God would have appeared in an earth-shattering way or as a mighty rushing wind. But for Elijah He came as a 'gentle whisper'. If you are expecting loud bangs and flashing lights each time you meet with God then you may miss the whisper. Conversely, if you expect the whisper only, then he may be in the sound of the trumpet or indeed in the voice from the burning bush.

> Now Moses was tending the flock of Jethro his father-in-law, the priest of Midian, and he led the flock to the far side of the desert and came to Horeb, the mountain of God. There the angel of the LORD appeared to him in flames of fire from within a bush. Moses saw that though the bush was on fire it did not burn up. So Moses thought, 'I will go over and see this strange sight – why the bush does not burn up.' When the LORD saw that he had gone over to look, God called to him from within the bush, 'Moses! Moses!' And Moses said, 'Here I am.' 'Do not come any closer,' God said. 'Take off your sandals, for the place where you are standing is holy ground.' Then he said, 'I am the God of your father, the God of Abraham, the God of Isaac and the God of Jacob.' At this, Moses hid his face, because he was afraid to look at God. (Exod. 3:1–6)

Our theological position or indeed prejudices about other types of

Christian spirituality may shape our expectations of God. We may miss out on a rich and wide spiritual life as the result of a cultural perspective that we have turned into a theology.

We are often most comfortable with the devotional style of the type of church we belong to or grew up in and may argue for its approach with great enthusiasm from a stance that could be nothing more than familiarity. I will never forget a prayer meeting that I had been involved in arranging for two groups of leaders from different church types that were theologically similar. It was a great meeting, with rich fellowship, but what stood out for me the most was the devotional culture of the two groups. One group began praying loudly, stamping around the room while shouting at God with a constant peppering of 'Yes God!' and 'Hallelujah!' The other group remained seated and quietly chose their words of prayer. Both groups were telling God and asking Him the same things but the adopted modes were different. I would have been deeply saddened if either group had suggested that their mode was the right one. Fortunately there was a good deal of acceptance of each other.

Case study

Sarah, a Baptist pastor of some twelve years' standing, began her Christian life in a conservative evangelical setting. As time went by, she entered into an experience that she and others termed 'charismatic' and her view of God in her life began to change. She adopted a new mode in her personal devotional life that now fitted her new understanding. Once again the years went by and she began to look to God for a more contemplative approach in her life with Him. Today Sarah is impossible to label. She holds to her 'charismatic experience' while worshipping in her devotional life with a burning candle and daily offices of prayer more in keeping with an earlier Celtic Christian spirituality. Sarah has had difficulty sharing her personal journey with others because she feels that she is expected to hold to a party line of one kind or another. She appeals for a greater acceptance of alternative approaches to spirituality.

Reflection

Do you consider yourself to have a wide view of the devotional life?

We will all have different expectations of God in our devotional lives. Some of these expectations will limit us, while others will expand us. Some of our expectations of God will have come to us from our theological perspectives, perhaps others from our prejudices.

Of self

A sense of failure or success with regard to the 'devotional life' is often the result of people's expectation of their own performance. Their expected performance will also be shaped by their held views. Such views come from a variety of sources.

St Augustine was greatly helped in his understanding of God and the devotional life by reading the testimony books of Christians such as Antony of Egypt. Many Christians today are encouraged in their faith by testimony books, but some find them overwhelmingly accusing as they attempt to measure their spiritual lives against the heroes of the faith. Stories about the prayer life of Martin Luther and of John Wesley abound. They suggest long hours, usually beginning very early in the morning, spent in prayer. The message they convey is, 'The harder you work for God in a day, the longer you must spend in prayer.' Many Christian workers attempt to live up to this but find themselves falling short and living with the tension of 'failing' an attractive spiritual ideal.

Case study

One young man heard a well-known speaker say in public that he had begun to get up early in the morning, around 5.00am, to pray, and that his life had benefited from this discipline. The young man was deeply impressed and attempted to copy this. He was always up early to go to work and so arranged to get up even earlier. He grew very tired, though he had made concerted attempts to get to bed earlier at night. The young man persevered and about a year later found himself in the home of the same well-known speaker. In conversation with the speaker's wife, he mentioned his attempts to emulate his hero. The speaker's wife was amazed because her husband had attempted this praying style for two weeks and then given it up. This young man had attempted to live up to the fantasy that his hero was succeeding, when in fact he had failed.

Guilt and failure seem to be lurking around the corner of each of our attempts to become great men and women of prayer. While I recognise the wide variety of views concerning the devotional life and spiritual warfare, I can't help thinking that much of the failure experienced is set up for us at the start, by embracing the devotional ideals of others without reference to our own time and our own lives.

Case study

Richard, a Methodist minister for three years, had looked forward to 'freedom' from secular employment in order to explore his relationship with God to the full. He had believed that part of the 'setting aside for ministry' would include increased opportunity for devotions. He began with great intentions but soon discovered that he felt overwhelmed with the responsibilities of his role. He found it increasingly difficult to find the time to pray and when he did find the time he didn't know where to start or how to organise the time allotted. Richard was invited to a seminar on prayer and discovered a tool that divided an hour into helpful segments that would structure an hour of prayer. This was a great help to him. He was able to fix an hour a day but soon needed more time, and took it. The seminar had helped him to order his busy life and gave structure to his devotions. Richard began to feel that he was reaching the aims he had started out with and was much encouraged.

It is possible for the lives and experiences of others to encourage or discourage us. Positive or negative modelling may lead to realistic expectations of ourselves or to feelings of failure as we build unrealistic expectations into our lives. It is possible to enter into bondage to a set of values that have been adopted from the perspectives of another. When the devotional life is joyless and a hard slog it is much less likely to be fulfilling and much more likely to become a source of guilt and self-condemnation.

Reflection

What influences do you recognise have been moulded into your devotional life? Have these influences been helpful?

Time

Just when is the best time for us to carry out our devotions? Should they be weekly, daily, hourly? If we were to survey a cross-section of Christians we would probably be encouraged to believe that the correct time was one of several strongly held positions.

Many people find that the suggested early morning 'quiet time' really doesn't work. First they are physically unable to withstand the earlier start, not because they are lazy, but because they live stress-filled lives and work long hours. Second they have five children and the house is never quiet.

Other people find the suggestion that we must pray longer if we are going to work harder impossible with the lifestyle experienced in the twenty-first century. It is true that in the West the working week has grown shorter and that the average family is better off financially than 100 or 200 years ago. However, the forward march of civilisation and of technology has brought a pressure to life that few can resist. Today the working day may be interrupted incessantly by the telephone ringing, by a demanding fax or by an email. A visit to the shop means being faced with a vast range of choices that need to be evaluated at the level of health, cost, and so on, as we stand in a long queue waiting to get out of the shop. A parcel can be (and therefore must be) sent to cross the Atlantic Ocean by tomorrow. A piece of work must be finished by the end of the day. The pace of life has speeded up. We now expect more productivity from less time. The more time we save with technology the more activity we can fit into our already crowded lives. We have lost the art of stillness and the beauty of silence. And as for the invention of the light bulb – great though it is, it has increased the length of our day.

Some of the great feats of praying by the Christians of old were possible only because it took them days to get, say, from London to York on the back of a horse, or weeks from England to America by ship. The slower pace of living increased the opportunity for longer hours spent in devotions. While life had its real hardships and a working day was longer, harder and less rewarding, time was used differently and was more conducive in some respects to silence, stillness and calm – those places where the devotional life can soar.

It is certainly true that time spent with God is essential and enormously beneficial for a healthy Christian life.

> Very early in the morning, while it was still dark, Jesus got up, left the house and went off to a solitary place, where he prayed. (Mark 1:35)

> After he had dismissed them, he went up on a mountainside by himself to pray. When evening came, he was there alone. (Matt. 14:23)

> But Jesus often withdrew to lonely places and prayed. (Luke 5:16)

In the above passages, Jesus demonstrates a preferred mode of personal devotion as He goes off alone to pray. It would appear that He did this often and at different times of the day. If we use Jesus as a role model, then His life seems to suggest that we should spend time alone with God. When, where, how long, seemed to fit in with the circumstances in which Jesus found Himself.

Consider these questions: Have we developed a spiritual 'rate of exchange'? Do we believe that the earliness of the morning when we pray, and the length of time spent, correlates directly to the extent of God's blessing in our lives?

Many people find that they pray best when the day is over and they are in bed relaxed; others find it better in the middle of the day. It would be better to discover the best times and places for your own devotional life than to attempt to fit your life into another person's preferences. What works for you will suit you best. What approach you take is a matter of personal choice.

The devotional life may also include the reading of Scripture. Once again, many views have been offered on the 'right' way to go about this. It is easy to fall into the 'rate of exchange' mentality again. The person who reads a book of the Bible each day may actually have less benefit from this approach than the person who reads a verse each week. Consider carefully the 'how' of reading Scripture so that it best fits your mind and heart. The 'how' of reading is of greater importance than the 'how much'.

The devotional life has some major aims: it aims to enhance your walk with God and enrich your Christian life. It aims to instruct you and help you to grow. It aims at enabling you to worship God and bring Him praise. It aims at intercession as we bring before God, people and situations in need of His touch. Any attempt at a definition will be shallow and fall short since it will be limiting.

Wherever you are on this 'aims continuum', the important thing is that you develop an approach that aids the fulfilment of your aims; that you are enabled and enriched by meeting with God and are fulfilled in your relationship with Him. The devotional life has become a 'religious chore' for many and they need to be given the freedom to begin to enjoy this rich opportunity.

Time is an aspect of the devotional life. If no time is given, then no devotional life is experienced and we are the worse for it. Any relationship needs the investment of time in order that it may be a healthy relationship.

The rhythm of life

It is important to retain the freedom to develop your own pattern of devotions because this will work best for you. Our lives work to a rhythm that has been developed over time. To fit into our own rhythm will cause us to escape the feelings of guilt and failure that can come from the adoption of another's rhythm.

The problem of discipline

This is a negative subtitle, as it immediately assumes that discipline is a problem. Many do in fact feel guilty because they lack the ability to order their working lives. When this is true, often the first area to suffer is the devotional life and this increases the experience of guilt. The word 'discipline' may bring to mind a number of negative pictures or memories of the past, particularly for those personality types that are more random in their approach to life. Discipline must be seen as a tool that enables us to meet our personal goals or aims. It has been a problem for many because they have sought to discipline themselves to another's aims and have failed. If we lack compatibility with the aims and style of another, then all the discipline in the world is not going to help us. We cannot become a square peg in a round hole.

Personality types

There is a temptation to believe that all people are the same and that what works for one will work for all. In a recent counselling session with a young pastor, I was able to witness the relief he experienced as he realised that he was different from others and that this was all right. A simple thing perhaps, but many people struggle with stereotypes, even though we are all unique and there are numerous categories of personality. Studies have shown that some people learn by touch and sight, while others learn textually. Some think in text, others in pictures. A problem with discipline may simply be a problem with living like someone else, and using the skills of a completely different personality. It is possible to discover our personality type by using tools like the Myers–Briggs test instruments, which can help us to become more self-aware. Self-awareness is not a form of introversion or misplaced self-interest; it is a 'seeing', 'freeing' exercise that enables us to approach our lives and relationships with a greater level of awareness and personal maturity. To know myself may help prevent me from attempting to be someone else.

Time management

The classic problem with attending seminars on time management is that we may lack the skills to make time to attend the seminar! We are all different in our use of time. We will have developed our habits with the use of time over many years and sometimes these are bad habits not easily broken. If we suffer from bad time habits, then our devotional life will be suffering along with it and we will be aware of this because of the negative feelings it gives us. We are often tempted to make huge attempts to correct these problems. When we make unrealistic New Year resolutions, we do well until 4 January when a tidal wave of failure sweeps over us, together with that sinking feeling that we will never be able to change. Good changes are often painstaking and take time to implement.

If you are having problems managing your time you might like to try the following:

- Read a book on time management
- Talk to a colleague
- Talk to your spouse
- Go to a seminar
- Develop a working model for your life

Whatever you do, plan to make one-step changes. A climber reaches the summit of the mountain by taking small steps, not giant leaps. Giant leaps have giant falls and the guilt and feelings of failure that attend us are the real enemies of the devotional life. Fortunately, when we come to Christ we are not issued with a clocking-in card by a God who considers our hours, but we come to Father who warmly welcomes us into His presence.

Motivation

Enjoyment is often the reason why we engage in a number of life's activities. It becomes a source of motivation for the enjoyable activity that follows. Other things, such as the need to achieve or the pursuit of promotion in a career, can also be a motivational force. There are a large number of motivators and each of us will be affected by a different range of them. One thing we all have in common is that we will act or react according to these forces.

Reflection

A good question to consider at this stage, then, is: What motivates me to engage in my devotional life?

The opposite of this thinking is also true. There are forces that also demotivate us to certain actions. A dislike of something or a feeling of fear or inadequacy may prevent us from carrying out an important task. Procrastination is often caused by negative demotivational forces that weigh so heavily upon us that we put off the task for as long as possible, sometimes to ridiculous lengths.

Reflection

Another helpful question to consider here is: What are the demotivational forces in my devotional life?

I am aware that enjoyment is probably not the driving force behind the needs and purposes of our devotional life. However, when something is a pleasure we tend to move towards it. I believe that with some adjustments based on our self-awareness, we can improve the motivational factors of our devotional life and that it can become a pleasure to engage in.

My Godview

My view and understanding of God will help to determine whether I am comfortable in my relationship with Him. The more relaxed I feel about

God, the easier it will be for me to approach Him in my devotional life.

Many people equate God with the most dominant figure they have experienced in their earlier lives. If this was a negative figure whom it was difficult to be close to, then this may affect the way we feel about God.

Case study

Alasdair had always looked up to his father but had never felt that he could get close to him. It didn't seem to matter how hard Alasdair worked at school, his results, often very good, were never good enough to please his father. An 85 per cent pass would invite questions about the other 15 per cent. Alasdair had grown used to this and had thought no more about it until he had entered the Anglican ministry. As a curate he had struggled hard with his devotional life and continually felt such a failure that his approach to people was always shy and guarded, in fear that he might be discovered, by people more spiritual than himself, to be a fraud.

Alasdair eventually went for counselling and came to realise that there was nothing wrong with his devotional life. He had found it hard to relate to God because he was projecting his own father image onto Him. He secretly believed that God, as a Father, would reject him and constantly find fault with him. However, once Alasdair realised that God was his heavenly Father, who warmly invited his presence, he went on to discover a new confidence in his ministry life and a freedom in his devotional life. He no longer approached his devotional life with fear and trepidation.

We may be demotivated out of a sense of a bruised or broken relationship with God. If we feel that in some way we have failed God and are unacceptable to Him, we may avoid our devotional lives out of a sense of shame. Like a vicious circle, we may miss out on time with God and then avoid Him because we feel bad about our devotions. Round and round it goes. Viewing God as seated in judgment may be a theological truth, but this Godview needs to be completed with an understanding of the pleasure that He takes in all of us as His children.

Comfort zones

We can call these aspects of motivation our 'comfort zones'; the avoidance of our devotional lives or perhaps more appropriately avoidance of God, since for one of numerous reasons we are not comfortable in coming close to Him. This can continue for years. It is possible to believe in God and in His forgiveness and yet to keep this in the back of our mind: accepting that ultimately we are saved and that God isn't going to change His mind, but having real difficulty in experiencing a day-by-day relationship. Feeling uncomfortable in our personal relationship with God may also lead to a 'doing' mentality or spirituality. Some people apply for and are accepted as ministerial or missionary candidates because they want to ease their sense of guilt by offering their lives in God's service. We could call this 'service through guilt'. These people are quite uncomfortable in their devotional lives and prefer a distant approach to worship and spirituality. They have never dealt with their guilt before God and feel too guilty to be close to Him. There is an almost subconscious belief that 'this angry God can be appeased by offering to serve Him'. Rarely do any of these people escape their feelings of guilt, even after long years of Christian service. The answer lies in the nature of the relationship and not in the offer of service.

How you view God and how you relate to Him seriously affects the nature of your devotional life, which can lie at the heart of the difference between engaging in the devotional life out of pleasure or doing so out of duty.

Method and innovation

One of the underlying themes of this section of the chapter has been the observation that we copy others in our approach to the devotional life. This is not an appeal for everyone to be original in their approach, as it is difficult for anything to be truly original and it would deny the good lessons we may learn from the lives of others. So the suggestion is that we discover an approach to the devotional life that works for us and provides us with what we need and are looking for.

Case study

Max is a police officer and drives police motor vehicles for many hours of his working life. During his driving course Max was repeatedly reprimanded for the use of his indicators when approaching a turning. He was using them every time and was told that this was incorrect. Max realised that he had been taught to do this and that not to do so would have resulted in a failed driving test. He questioned the police instructor over this matter. Max was told only to use the indicators when there were other road users present. This would keep him fresh and observant and would save him from becoming a habitual driver. The habitual driver was seriously disadvantaged and would not remain fresh and fully observant.

This is good advice. Our devotional lives can become stale and lacking in effectiveness if they are conducted with a sense of habit. I would strongly encourage a varied approach to our devotions. This thinking is alternative to much that is taught about devotions. Many favour the habitual approach because it develops a rhythm of life that will help us to maintain our devotional life. I can understand this but I believe that it is better if people discover the best pattern, in terms of time, for their daily devotions and that they vary the content or approach.

I resist the temptation to become one more voice offering the best way for you to carry out your devotional life, so this section of the chapter is not designed to be a catalogue of devotional methods. However, I suggest that we involve a good measure of creativity in what we do to provide the freshness so often lacking. What follows will be a number of considerations concerning creative approaches to the devotional life.

This same exercise is included in the course upon which this book has been based. It is offered here as a helpful tool for reflecting on your devotional experience.

Write a list of the different component parts of your existing devotional approach in a similar way to the example below:

1. Prayers of adoration
2. Prayers of confession
3. Prayers of thanksgiving
4. Songs of praise
5. Songs of reflection
6. Songs of worship
7. Prayers of intercession
8. Read the scripture devotionally

9. Read the scripture instructionally
10. Read devotional material
11. Read instructional material
12. Enjoy silence
13. Listen
14. Meditate
15. Play some background music
16. Listen to background sounds
17. Play some testimony tapes
18. Listen to the Bible on cassette
19. Read or write a poem
20. Dig in the garden
21. Walk in a field
22. Fly a kite
23. Sail a boat
24. Tackle a hard physical (but not mental) task
25. Shout into the wind
26. Stare at the fish
27. Pet the dog
28. Feel some stones
29. Go to the art gallery
30. Smell the flowers

This is not offered as a complete list or a list to aspire to. Your list may be longer or shorter and completely different.

Make your list and look at it for a while. Now put it into the kind of order you prefer. You may then want to experiment with the order of things. Ask yourself if this is a fulfilling list and add or subtract as necessary.

Keep your list for future reflection.

You may want to experiment with some aspects of the devotional life from my list above. Look at your list and ask yourself which of the component parts fit into these three categories:

1. Worship of God
2. Feeding my own soul
3. Fulfilling my Christian duty

It may not be easy to make clear decisions about this since there can be overlap in these areas. These different categories represent 'inflows' and 'outflows' and we are looking for a good balance in both.

Multiple-component devotions

People often lump together their entire devotional requirement in one session, rattling through it all like an express train. Of course this is fine if you like it like that, but the speed of life makes stillness difficult to achieve. Away from the 'rat race', this is the one place where time stands still and you are alone with God: 'Be still, and know that I am God' (Psa. 46:10). This verse becomes a haunting ideal that few feel they can experience.

Single-component devotions

This is not to suggest that we don't involve ourselves in each of the basic areas of our devotional life, but that we do not bring them all together at one time. We may try focusing on one area during one devotional session. We may try using more than one aspect, but at different times of the day or week. Play around with it a little!

Simplicity and complexity

Case study

Brian, a Free Church minister, was embarking upon a week-long retreat at a quiet beauty spot where he would have a room to himself in peaceful surroundings. He asked my advice about the content of his retreat and told me that he was taking along his Bible and several other Christian books. I asked Brian if he was hoping for the opportunity to catch up with his reading while on retreat. He hadn't set this as a target, but was just making sure that he had enough material to fill the time.

Brian was surprised when I suggested he leave his books behind. He was anxious about the 'time' aspect. How would he fill it? He was even more anxious when I suggested that he leave his Bible behind. He felt that I was going too far with this suggestion and that it was his Christian duty to have his Bible with him at all times. I went on to suggest that he select one verse only, and that he might spend the week quietly with God thinking and meditating on this verse. Brian decided to take this advice and came back refreshed with the realisation that quality can be better than quantity when it came to the reading of Scripture. He realised that he had been afraid of listening and had found it easier to fill his devotional times with activity. He had been blessed by a new experience of stillness and simplicity.

The devotional life is not an examination to pass or fail. We can dare to take liberties with it and experiment. Simplicity can often be profound where complexity can be just too crowded.

An exercise I have asked Christian leaders in several countries to engage in is not profound so much as illustrative. Take a moment now and stop what you are doing. Sit back in your chair with your eyes closed:

- What are you aware of?
- What can you hear?
- Listen to everything around you.

Practise this stillness. I have discovered that for many people the silence is crowded at first. Our minds can be filled with so much that all we can hear is the echo of our inner being. But this passes. I think we descend from quietness into silence and stillness through practice and the giving of time to this kind of exercise.

I once asked a congregation to spend fifteen minutes in silence, just listening. They found it difficult to be still for 'such a long time'. We often feel the need to fill silence as if silences were empty. The little exercise above should show you that silence is far from empty and sometimes far from silent.

Students taking my course are asked to set aside a whole day and find a comfortable place, preferably a quiet one, to spend the whole day in silence. They use the time to think and reflect on the thoughts and feelings this chapter has brought to the surface, and to consider their devotional life and how it may become a richer experience. Why don't you try this too?

Here's another exercise you may want to try. Take some time and look at the words below. Circle the ones you most feel describe your current experience of the devotional life. Add to the list any other words that seem appropriate. Use them in your next devotional time as items for prayer and/or praise.

Rush/Pressure/Noise/Hurry/Quiet/Peace/
Complex/Simple/Fear/Pain/Joy/Security/
Loud/Slow/Fast/Full/Empty/Words/Songs/
Whisper/Drowning/Flying/Soaring/Climbing/
Crawling/Running/Jumping/Crying/Laughing/
Feeling/Sadness/Happiness/Euphoric/Tired/
Insecure/Helpless/Dry/Fluid/Fruitful/Dull

One of the most helpful theological concepts for me is that of God's self-revelation through, in part, the created order. This tells me that I can see something of Him just by looking around me and taking note of what I see. One of the great sadnesses of this present age, particularly in the Western world, is that society is in such a hurry that it sees the concrete and not the roses. Things are taken so seriously that stress-beating light-heartedness is a thing of the past for many. A God who makes the face of a camel or the body of a moose must have a humorous streak! It seems as though a sense of well-being can be experienced with a God who creates smiles and laughter as part of our human make-up.

I love this poem and use it often:

If I had my life to live over again,
I'd try to make more mistakes next time:
I would relax, I would limber up, I would be sillier than I have been this trip.
I know of very few things I would take seriously.
I would take more trips, I would be crazier …
I would eat more ice cream and less beans
I would have more actual troubles and fewer imaginary ones.
You see I'm one of those people who lives life prophylactically and sensibly hour after hour, day after day.
Oh, I've had my moments, and if I had to do it over again, I'd have more of them …[1]

We have been considering method and innovation and their place in the devotional life. Whatever your preferred method or style, remember that this chapter has not set out simply to list methods, since this may be fulfilled by a selection of materials from any good Christian bookshop.

9. Recognising Burnout in the Ministry

As the writer of this book, let me say that I have professional qualifications in theology, counselling and pastoral studies, but not in medicine. What follows is as the result of my study and research on the subject of burnout and the symptoms that are widely reported.

Descriptive terms can be a problem but it is difficult to do without them. I am adopting the term 'burnout', which, although used and abused as a term, has a clear clinical definition. As a young police officer, in what seems like another lifetime, I was shocked by the attitude colleagues had for an inspector at our police station who had gone through what was then termed a 'nervous breakdown'. He was looked on with suspicion and concern, with many fellow officers wondering if he could now be trusted to perform well under pressure. This amounted to gross ignorance of the nature of stress and overstress and its causes and effects. What follows is an attempt to encourage you into a deeper understanding of the nature of stress and overstress that leads to burnout.

Stress is a part of living. The application of stress means placing something under tension, positively or negatively. Bridges are stressed to produce their incredible strength. Concrete cores are stressed to build rigidity into buildings. Strings are placed under stress to produce the beautiful music of the piano, violin and harp. Stress cannot be avoided, whether it is found in an object or in a person. Without the presence of stress, the fight or flight response in human beings would not operate. The adren-aline would not engage inside us to cause us to flee from threatened or imminent danger. Stress is here to stay!

Psychologist Archibald Hart has this to say as he describes the biological effects of stress:

> What happens is that the brain sends messages along two separate pathways. The first is to the pituitary gland, which releases a substance called 'adrenocorticotrophic hormone' or ACTH for short. ACTH in turn stimulates the adrenal glands.

> (The term *adrenal* literally means 'toward kidney,' from the Latin *ad renal*. The glands were so named because one is located on top of each kidney.) The second pathway is through the brain stem and spinal cord, which send nerve impulses to many parts of the body, including the adrenal glands. The combined effect of these chemical and neural signals is to stimulate the two major parts of the adrenal gland – the 'core' and the 'cortex.' The cortex releases many hormones, but the two important ones are cortisol and cortisone, both of which, at normal levels of arousal, help fight pain and inflammation. It is the core that releases adrenalin and noradrenalin into the bloodstream; these hormones stimulate the heart, raise the blood pressure, and prepare us for the unique emergency reaction in the body to which I have already alluded – the 'fight or flight' response. We are physically prepared either to attack the source of our stress or to run away from it. The effect of this 'fight or flight' response on the rest of the body is extremely important to understand. If we follow this response through its intricate and intertwined pathway, we can readily see how the various symptoms of prolonged stress are created. The increased demand for blood in the brain (to mobilize us for action) means that the *heart* has to do extra work; the *muscles* (to provide a quick getaway or more force in fighting) and the *stomach* (to digest food and provide needed energy.)[1]

'Fight or flight' is a common phrase used in various books when describing the condition of stress. It is clear that there are times when this union of emotion and physiology can be essential, when fleeing from potential harm or preparing for a difficult confrontation. However, stress as a prolonged experience means that the body is in this heightened state to the detriment of health and function. The following extract suggests that stress can cause wear on the vital organs of the body, thereby contributing to a person's death.

> Among all my autopsies (and I have performed well over a thousand), I have never seen a person who died of old age. In fact, *I do not think anyone has died of old age yet*. To permit this would be the ideal accomplishment of medical research ... To die of old age would mean that all the organs of the body had worn out proportionately, merely by having been used too long. This is never the case. We invariably die because one vital part has worn out too early in proportion to the rest of the body. The lesson seems to be that, as far as man can regulate his life by voluntary actions,

he should seek to equalize stress throughout his being! The human body – like the tires on a car, or the rug on a floor – wears longest when it wears evenly.[2]

Friedman and Rosenman, cardiologists who identified the personality-type most prone to heart disease, clearly indicate from their research the connection between prolonged adrenalin-arousal and heart disease. They state:

This is more or less what happens in the heart when there is a prolonged and chronic elevation of adrenalin. The adrenalin keeps the system moving at a high speed, and deterioration occurs at a faster rate. We actually age faster.

However, since an elevated adrenalin level can also give a person a heightened sense of well being, increased energy, reduced need for sleep, and feelings of excitement or even euphoria, we are often completely un-aware that this destruction is taking place. It is easy to see why many become addicted to this state of arousal. The feelings of security it provides can give one a dangerously false sense of well being.

Once more: The most serious effect of elevated adrenalin, when persistent and unrelenting, is its damage to the heart and arteries. The chronic excess discharge and circulation of the catecholamines (adrenalin and noradrenalin) may be the chief factor in the total process of arterial decay and thrombosis. We have seen coronary heart disease erupt in many subjects whose blood insulin levels and metabolism of cholesterol, fat, and sugar were quite normal. But rarely have we ever witnessed the onset of this disease in a person whose rate of manufacture and secretion of catecholamines (adrenalin and noradrenalin) we did not know or suspect to have been increased.[3]

It is fairly clear, then, that stress when experienced for a prolonged period is a serious health hazard. Davies, also quoting from the biologist Hans Selye, who was writing on stress in the 1960s, adds:

Dr Selye would distinguish three stages by which stress may lead to illness or breakdown. These are:

1. A stage of *alarm*: the signals were obvious that John's job was at risk, and he registered these with alarm.

2. A stage of *resistance*: he mobilises his resources to try and solve the problem that losing his job will pose for him and his family.
3. A stage of *exhaustion*: the threat arrives and is worse than he expected. For the time being he cannot cope and his physical health collapses.[4]

There is no doubt that stress is normal, but that the over-stressing of a person or object leads to collapse. Stress may be labelled 'positive stress' or 'negative stress'. This simply means that a person may be in a state of adrenalin arousal for pleasant reasons, like moving to a new house or catching an aeroplane for a holiday abroad, but is still experiencing the body's chemical exchanges. A person may also be in this state for unpleasant reasons, like having gone through a difficult experience or through prolonged and pressured work. In either case, too much stress can lead to breakdown, or worse.

Stress levels ought to be in the control of the individual. A person must learn to adjust stresses according to their perceived need. In order to do this, a person must learn to be in touch with their stressors or stress factors. These stressors are the stressful aspects of chosen activity and the way it is responded to.

Reflection

Are you aware of living in a stressed state for prolonged periods of time? Are you aware that fun, though pleasurable and helpful in many other ways, can also be a source of stress?

Many Christian leaders minister around the world, serving fruitfully with healthy working boundaries in place, which can be both positive and fulfilling. However, where a set of unrealistic expectations that lead to a working life that has lost a healthy balance exists, stress will inevitably take its toll on the sufferer. Often that toll is called 'burnout', a term used indiscriminately by a number of professions to describe a condition that prevents individuals from functioning to the acceptable levels of their profession.

There appear to be a number of similarities between burnout and depression, although the two terms are not synonymous. While burnout may include a period of depression, it is possible to suffer from an experience of burnout without being depressed and to be depressed without being burned out.

Burnout has been little understood by some and discredited by others, who regard it as highly suspect. However, it has been recognised professionally as a condition that particularly, though not exclusively, affects those in the caring professions.

Freudenberger popularised the term 'burnout' in 1980 and called it 'the high cost of aiming too high'.[5] This section of the chapter focuses specifically on conditions leading to burnout faced by those in the full-time Christian ministry.

Defining burnout

I begin by considering various definitions of burnout. Here are several descriptions:

> Burnout is the result of constant or repeated emotional pressure associated with an intense involvement with people over long periods of time. Such intense involvement is particularly prevalent in health, education and social service occupations, where professionals have a 'calling' to take care of other people's psychological, social and physical problems. Burnout is the realisation that they no longer can help people in need, that they have nothing left in them to give.[6]

This description suggests that there is a high incidence of burnout within the caring professions. Also that a sense of 'calling' may be a factor worthy of consideration.

Fineman describes how caring feels, as a symptom of burnout; that somehow the sufferers are unable to connect with the needs of others because of the blindness caused by their own prevalent need.

> Burnout – (a) a state of emotional and physical exhaustion, with a lack of concern for the job and a low trust of others, (b) a depersonalisation of clients; a loss of caring and cynicism towards them, and (c) self deprecation and low morale and a deep sense of failure.[7]

Rush links the experience of burnout with the feelings of failure and exhaustion that one may experience when efforts are not rewarded with success in relationships or tasks:

> Burnout can be defined as the type of stress and emotional fatigue, frustration and exhaustion that occurs when a series of (or combination of) events in a relationship, mission, way of life, or job, fail to produce an acceptable result.[8]

Sanford emphasises the destructive nature of burnout; that there has been a consumption of the whole person taking place. Energy has literally been burned up.

> If we apply the dictionary definition of burnout to human beings, we must imagine a man or woman who has been devoured from within by fiery energy until, like a gutted house, nothing is left. The word 'burnout' is drawn from the imagery of fire, and fire is a form and symbol for energy. So in its broadest scope, the problem of burnout is a problem of energy.[9]

Burnout is described by many as an experience of exhaustion. I would describe burnout as:

> The exhausting of the inner resource that enables a carer to go on caring. The using up of the essential 'inner you', rendering the individual in a serious condition of disfunctionality. The spending of self on others in such a way that the 'inner bank balance' has gone into the red.

I use this last phrase intentionally, because I equate burnout with self-awareness and personal management. I consider that burnout may be experienced if our sense of call and mission about the caring task consumes us to the extent that we become out of touch or unable to look after our own inner needs.

The words from a prayer by Ignatius of Loyola, 'to give and not to count the cost', are in one sense admirable, but in another wasteful, if the carer's ability to care is impaired by the lack of self-care. Ignatius was writing in the fifteenth century and was unaware of the stresses that may be faced by ministers in the twenty-first century. With regard to the professional Christian minister I consider that damage often occurs as the result of this approach. We *do* need to 'count the cost'.

Common sources of stress in ministry

Before moving further into the discussion of burnout, I want simply to list some of the most common sources of ministry stress. Even as I write I am aware that lists are never really complete and so let me suggest that you add to the list those things that are missing and that cause you to be stressed. Your own list will serve you well as you seek to understand better some of your experiences in the ministry:

When the day is done ...

Many occupations have a working day with a start and a finish. Some occupations, and the ministry is one of them, do not have a finish in that there can be a sense in which the minister is 'on call'. This can be taken to the extreme, though, by church and minister alike. The never-ending day is a source of stress since the mind may have trouble switching from work to leisure.

One more Christmas ...

Many ministers receive great joy from their preaching and from the Christian year, but in lengthy pastorates it can be stressful to continue to minister throughout the year with freshness. Preaching regularly in the same church (sometimes twice or three times a week) needs to be understood as energy-draining since each sermon has a huge creative requirement. Many ministers are under stress to continue this level of regular and heavy output.

So, you're back again ...

Much of the work of the minister is taken up with people, and many ministers enjoy this aspect. For some, it may even form part of the attraction to the role. Stress can result from having to give time to people who rarely act on the advice sought and just keep coming back for more of the same advice.

Black holes ...

I don't like using this description of people but it is a graphical image. Stress is experienced in the ministry when having to minister regularly to needy people who consume every last ounce of your time and energy and that of anyone within a ten-mile radius. These people have deep-seated needs that probably require different professional disciplines to those of the minister, but often ministers, for the good of the gospel, keep pouring out their energies.

Working with people ...

This is often highly energy-draining. Some ministers have spent the whole day with people, listening, comforting, interacting, and arrive home wondering why they are tired.

I don't build tables ...

If ministers did build tables then they would have something to view, a result to see. The role of Christian leader includes not always being able to know whether they have achieved anything.

Star Trek makes me cry ...

A minister attending one of my seminars offered some thoughts when I was discussing exposure to trauma. He told me that he had burst into tears while watching his favourite television programme, *Star Trek*, and had not known why until I had said that ministers are drained of emotional energy by dealing with the joys and sorrows of their members. A minister can typically be at a hospital bedside in the morning celebrating the joy of new birth with parishioners, take a funeral in the afternoon, and be at an eightieth birthday party in the evening. The minister may experience emotional pendulum swings in the course of a day or a week that are exhausting. My 'Trekkie' friend had experienced a number of weeks in a row just like this and finally his own emotional reserves collapsed into tears.

In the thick of it alone ...

Another major source of ministry stress is the fact that many ministers work alone, carrying a great sense of responsibility, shouldering the secret stories of church members entrusted in confidence, and feeling the burden of loneliness.

Where he goes, egos ...

This title stretches things a little, but ministers function in a role that may cause them to have a 'public face', the one they wear outside the house to depict their role. Wearing masks in public, while very common, saps energy reserves.

I should have been a fireman ...

Some ministers enjoy the need to be needed and encourage an 'I'm always available' motif within the church. Feeding emotionally on the late night calls and the 'It's only me' day-off phone calls is all very well, but the cost in stress is high. The fireman approach to ministry is ultimately destructive to the minister and their family. The rush and tear of the 'emergency minister' may be intoxicating but is dangerous.

Where should I be now ...?

Ministering in one church is stressful but a number of denominations require their ministers to serve multiple congregations. This is enormously draining and can be survived only with adequate personal stress management.

So, I'm not married ...

It would be remiss, when looking at ministry stress, not to include the lot of the single minister. Single ministers experience additional specific stressors: Matchmaking – church members believing that you should be married and they know just to whom! You have more time – where church members expect far more from you since you do not need to spend time with your immediate family. Less pay – in some church settings ministers are paid less if they are single, creating serious 'worth issues' for some single ministers.

From the city to the fields ...

Any discussion on stress in the ministry needs to take note that changing ministry locations can often mean having to cope with sharp cultural shifts. This is a steep learning curve that delivers further stress.

The new kid on the block ...

High stress levels are experienced when a minister moves to a new church: the sea of new faces, the attendant matrix of expectations, the settling-in 'honeymoon', the 'our last minister did it this way' comments, etc. This complex group of stressors needs to be kept in mind.

Where will we put the sideboard . . . ?
Moving pastorates often means moving house. No two ministry houses are the same shape and size. Ministering families often go through high stress trying to make the 'fit' into the new accommodation.

The list could go on and on and these things don't look so bad when viewed on their own – just normal stressful dynamics – but it all changes when you string a few together and repeat them week after week. Stressors accumulate and stress continues to exist in our system if no action is taken to alleviate the situation.

Reflection

Review the above list and any additions you have made, and consider what steps you could take to dissipate your stress levels.

As we look more closely now at burnout, I will discuss the subject further under the following headings:

- Causes of burnout
- Symptoms of burnout
- Effects of burnout

Causes of burnout

Burnout involves the overstressing of one's inner resources until those inner resources are used or burned up.

Too much
In terms of stress, a human being could be compared to a wooden stick or a metal bar. We can take a load, but too much will cause us to break. Christian ministers are largely left to work out the components of their working lives on their own. They are trusted with their time and left

to monitor their own workload. This is a privilege, but also a cause for concern because of the very nature of the work. Carers of any kind are compassionate by nature, motivated by the needs of others and go to great lengths to ease the burdens of the needy. There are innumerable needy people!

Case study

Dr Harrison, struggling with the entangled mass of vegetation, suddenly broke through into a clearing. The going felt easier now. He brushed himself down, feeling as though he had brought the jungle with him on his clothing. He looked around and realised that a few hundred yards ahead was a tribal village. It wasn't marked on the map but he knew that on his journey to meet the survey team where he would work as a team medic he would pass through areas reputed to be sparsely populated by a remote tribe. He had stumbled on the village quite by chance. These people were known to be friendly but preferred to live miles from anyone else. As he made his way into the village he was greeted by several tribesmen who were waving and shouting with broad grins on their small round faces.

Dr Harrison received a tremendous welcome from a people who rarely meet any outsiders. He was encouraged by their natural generosity and warmth of spirit but his attention was taken by the physical condition of a high percentage of those gathered round him. Many were lame or blind, and several had disfigured faces from the ravages of disease. He opened his medical bag and got to work.

Soon many of the tribespeople were gathered around in the hope that they too would be eased by this kind man's medicine. These people were in great need and were far from any other help. Dr Harrison reached deep into himself and thought to himself, 'These people are suffering greatly and I can help them, but I am due at the survey site very soon to take up my post. What shall I do?'

Caring for people is a never-ending task. Those who engage in this activity professionally are in great danger of burnout if they attempt to take on too much. Such people have a strong desire to help and go about their work with enthusiasm and a passion that sometimes borders on compulsion. Christian ministers are doubly at risk because of their spiritual perspectives. They believe that the unbeliever can die at any time and that their soul may be lost for all eternity. They carry out their role with a passion and urgency, attempting to fulfil passages such as: 'Preach the Word; be prepared in season and out of season; correct, rebuke and encourage – with great patience and careful instruction' (2 Tim. 4:2).

It becomes difficult for ministers to know when they should stop for a while. In some cases, they may not know how to stop, because their hearts are so full of the needs of others and the call of God. The needs of others begin to outweigh their personal needs. This is not a theological criticism of such beliefs, but is an observation of how they may influence behaviour.

Too often

Another area of overstress concerns ministers who are available for others too often. We can see this at work in several areas:

Lost balance

The high ideals of the Christian ministry fill the minister with such a sense of purpose that the individual may lose sight of their own humanity. An almost martyr-like approach may be adopted that often results in burnout and in complete physical, emotional and marital breakdown – and in family dysfunctionality.

The long-distance runner focuses on the end of the race and on finishing it before anyone else. The less experienced runner does the same, but assumes that winning means being the first away from the starting block. However, they may soon be exhausted after spending too much energy in the first half of the race. The struggling runner may suffer the indignity of watching the more experienced and paced runners glide past to a triumphant finish.

The Christian minister who learns to pace his or her working life will work better for longer than the one who rushes to save everyone as quickly as possible. Collectively, the paced worker produces more in the long run, although they may be criticised by others for their seeming lack of passion.

Motivation

It is considered honourable to be motivated by the needs of others, possibly as the result of interpreting biblical teaching on self-sacrifice, service and selflessness, or perhaps from the study of Christians from history, such as Francis of Assisi who embraced 'Mother Poverty' as a major aspect of his spirituality. Many ministers are seen as heroes if they expend themselves on their work. They are applauded for their sense of urgency and their grasp of human need.

Ministers can become like firemen who respond to the emergency call, regardless of who makes it, or when. They are off to help in the dead of night, frequently to a person who has been wrestling with their problems for several years and for whom a few more hours would make little difference. While crisis control is sometimes required, emergencies are in reality few. Ministers who are heading for burnout are often unable to distinguish a genuine emergency from a false one. These ministers are loved for the attention they give until, as the result of too much effort, they crash headlong into their own needs.

They should instead pull back, as they are in desperate need of rest and relaxation. They are no longer able to offer this high level of service. It is at times like this that the 'needy' become the 'angry', as they have been encouraged to have unrealistic expectations of their minister. They may want their hero to minister to them and do not expect this figure to have to deal with personal needs.

In a recent speaking trip to a group of Baptist ministry couples in the USA, a couple asked to speak to my wife and me, after spending part of the previous seminar session in tears. They told us a tragic story. They had lost their teenage daughter ten years before in a road accident.

The church they served as minister and wife asked them not to display their emotions, because their daughter was now in heaven and the church needed their help to get over the trauma. This couple had accepted the terrible responsibility and had been slowly eroded by unexpressed grief and pain through the ensuing years. They were able to make use of the moment to weep and begin a journey of recovery after years of inhuman and misguided suffering. They had been motivated towards the needs of others but had gone beyond the level where human health remains intact.

Honest self-appraisal

It is important for ministers to check within themselves and ask serious questions about their motivation for ministry. The need to be needed is a basic human requirement and everyone in the ministry will share this dynamic. Indeed, this motivational force can be the seedbed that leads to a life in the ministry. However, the ministry may attract those who do not in natural ways achieve their sense of being needed and put this personal essential into their professional lives instead. There can exist a mismatch between the personal and the professional.

Reflection

Ask yourself this honest question: Are my motives centred in:

- God?
- Others?
- Self?

Too little

Imagine digging up a field with a teaspoon. Church leaders who are facing burnout have been undertaking a huge task with limited resources. They may have begun with vast resources, but have used them up. When we work in an unhealthy way, we burn up our inner resources.

Ministry life can be compared to a bank account. A bank account is a good thing when it is kept solvent. However, we run into problems when we keep withdrawing money without depositing any. Eventually, the account goes into the red and there is no money left. Ministers can find themselves drawing on their inner reserves of strength, energy, belief system, and so on, until they have nothing left. Often the flow is one way – out! Typically, there may be too many evenings out, too many hurried meals, too many cancelled days off, too little time spent with family, too little time for self, and too many telephone calls. And so the list continues. One of the major causes of burnout is doing too much with little in return to offset the balance of inner resources. John Hillman describes this condition in McCormick's work:

> We are led by medicine itself, through its own notion of health, to live beyond ourselves, driven and exhausted, in threat of breakdown, owing to the denial of human frailty. When the physician cautions to slow down, his own 'go, go, go' and 'furor agendi' prevents his warnings from having effect. 'Getting better' means 'getting stronger'; health has become

> equivalent to strength, strength to life. We are built up to break down and then be rebuilt as we were before, like a machine caught in accelerated feedback. The soul seems to make itself heard only by speaking the physician's language – symptoms.[10]

This aiming beyond humanity is a common aspect for those who have experienced or are experiencing burnout. Many ministers find themselves digging deep into their hearts, searching for one more sermon. Preaching a sermon is a spiritual activity, possibly an academic activity, and certainly an emotional activity. It burns emotional energy, but is also a creative activity. Creativity requires space and peace, aspects of life that give back instead of taking out.

Case study

Martin found himself looking up old sermons in the hope that he could come up with one that the congregation wouldn't remember. He had spent days trying to prepare something fresh. He didn't feel that God had spoken to him or that anything fresh was forthcoming. He had found himself doing this for some weeks. When he had entered the ministry he promised himself that he would not use old material (not necessarily a problem unless you prefer not to). He had been feeling exhausted with his routine of six days and five evenings spent working. His devotional life had been suffering greatly and he had begun to feel like a production line for sermons, talks and studies. Everything was going out, and little was coming in. Martin felt a deep sense of failure. He felt as if he were a fraud, pretending to bring a message to the congregation while going through the motions in reality. Preaching had lost its feel of joy and excitement. He was troubled and didn't know how to stop the cycle of events because he was a 'minister' and this was 'the job'.

McBurney writes: 'I find that burnout results from trying to meet demands that are perceived to be greater than one's ability to meet them.'[11]

Too late

When considering the large number of stressors faced by those in full-time Christian ministry, it is possible to say that the minister's role is stressful. If ministers do not heed the warnings or think carefully about their approach to this role and other caring roles, then it is possible that they will burn out in the ministry. They will become used up and empty, and their physical, spiritual and emotional health will suffer.

The following is a story given to me by a well-known evangelist and author about his own experience:

Case study

In the summer of 1987 I prepared a talk for an American radio station on 'stress'.

> Stress is the great killer, an assassin so skilled in the art of destruction that each of us is at risk. The rapid acceleration of technology, the competitive nature of our society, the fixation with success, and the fear of redundancy and unemployment have created an environment in which stress can stalk unhindered ... Tragically, Christians are not immune to this new menace. Each year thousands of sincere Christian leaders are killed or wounded by stress-related disorders. The rest and peace that Christ promised has eluded them.

Several weeks after recording this chillingly prophetic message, I collapsed at a youth conference. The doctor suspected a brain haemorrhage. My blood pressure had risen alarmingly and only a strong heart and my fitness kept me from a cardiac crisis. What were the factors that led to this problem?

1. I had imbibed the Western myth that a person's value is determined by achievement. If each second of my day was not spent in the work of God, I felt guilty and inadequate.
2. I was working far too hard, attempting to achieve more than I was capable of doing. My success as an evangelist was measured by a full diary. I was a victim of the hedonism of work.
3. Ordinarily, I would rise early in the morning to meet with God. This time was slowly being eroded by the pressure of work and responsibilities. The activities of a very busy life were intruding into the most exalted and sublime activity: intimacy with God.

4. The neglect of my relationship with God found its counterpart in the neglect of my body. It had been my practice for some years to spend at least an hour each day in weight training, cycling, running or some other cardiovascular exercise. My fitness and physical strength had enabled me to be mentally and physically resilient. The demands of a busy ministry encroached on this time and press-ups, bench presses and trunk curls were replaced by committee meetings and preaching engagements. I was running helter-skelter towards the assassin and didn't know it.
5. I ignored God's command to take a Sabbath of rest. Without a day of reflection and relaxation, my judgment was impaired. I had no opportunity to be silent, to reflect on my life and the quality of my work. The irony of my predicament is not lost on me. The fact that I could write so perceptively about stress, yet be suffering from the same condition I described, shows how remote I was from reality.
6. I had always secretly believed in my indestructibility. I could abuse my body, neglect regular patterns of sleep and fix indefinitely on adrenaline without any serious consequences. And then suddenly I was staring into the eyes of the assassin, looking into the barrel of his gun. Bang! I was as vulnerable and weak as any other man, just another wounded Christian leader who'd played Superman once too often.

For many of us it is too late to avoid burnout: it has happened. The next chapter in this book points to some possible ways of recovering from this.

Symptoms of burnout

For our purposes here I will next describe some of the more obvious symptoms and consider them in three basic areas:

- Physical symptoms
- Emotional symptoms
- Spiritual symptoms

We should remember, as we approach this material, that human nature has a tendency to reflect symptoms upon itself. Like the character in the comic classic *Three Men in a Boat*, we may read a medical dictionary and imagine that we are suffering from every recorded ailment.

Physical symptoms of burnout

Burnout, as a response to overstress and collective stress, involves a number of different physical symptoms. People also react differently to different stimuli. When anxious, for example, some people lose their appetite, and others can't stop eating; some people pace the floor, while others flop on a couch.

What follows is a list of possible symptoms, which are widely reported in the literature available. Rush illustrates this by describing a syndrome that he calls the 'Elijah-decision', after the story in the Bible from 1 Kings 19, where the prophet Elijah is in the depths of despair and wishes to die:

> The Elijah-decision represents the depths of burnout. It is the culmination of the following major consequences of burnout:
>
> - Loss of purpose in life
> - Having one's self-image destroyed
> - Feeling alone in the world
> - Being filled with resentment and bitterness
> - Feeling that all is hopeless
>
> There are certainly other consequences of burnout that could be listed. However, these represent the major factors that contribute to a person's arriving at the decision to give up on life and eventually wish he or she was dead.[12]

Fatigue or tiredness

A constant state of tiredness not alleviated by regular sleep patterns. One's energy is dissipated to such an extent that the smallest task seems difficult.

Weight problems

People may gain a lot of weight over a short period of time as they eat to comfort their inner being. No amount of eating will improve the problem, but people commonly respond in this way. Conversely, people may begin to lose weight as they struggle with their problems, because they lose interest in food.

Physical pain
Some people may suffer from regular headaches. Others experience low back pain from the tension retained within their muscles. Yet others may suffer with stomach problems. They may experience pain and bouts of diarrhoea. Limbs may ache as the result of muscular tension brought on by the stress. Some people suffer pain in the centre of the chest and are worried that they are having a heart attack. It is important to get these things checked by a doctor, but they are often stress responses.

Loss of sleep
Insomnia; vivid dreams; difficulty in staying asleep; loss of perspective; small problems becoming large in the mind as the mind churns over the concerns that you have.

High anxiety state
Burnout may be attended by heightened anxiety as the sufferer responds to fears and qualms. High anxiety can cause the heart to beat faster, a tightening in the chest, sharp head pains, sweating on the forehead and palms, and can cause the face to be flushed and the limbs to shake.

Raised blood pressure
The sufferer may experience a rise in blood pressure.

Hurry sickness
Dr Archibald D. Hart, in his book *The Hidden Link Between Adrenalin and Stress*, discusses the problem of hurry sickness. More accurately, adrenaline addiction. Stress produces a surge of adrenaline in our body as it prepares for 'fight or flight'. This surge can feel like a motivating rush. Many Christian ministers work from this heightened position, believing it to be indicative of the presence of the Holy Spirit. The constant experience of this rush can lead to an addiction to pressure. Strange as it may sound, we can become addicted to hurry and pace. Sufferers may find themselves rushing everywhere like an emergency vehicle racing to put out some non-existent fire or to perform some fictitious rescue. They will find themselves eating faster than other family members or colleagues. They may be tempted to finish the sentences of others who are making a point slowly. They do everything as if the world were about to end within the next ten minutes. This condition can contribute to being burned out.

Sexual problems

Sufferers may experience a heightened interest in sexual activity as an attempt to comfort themselves in the face of their problems. Once again, the opposite may be true and sufferers may have low sexual desire coupled with low energy. In some cases they may experience impotency.

Skin conditions

The sufferer may experience some skin complaints such as soreness, itching or flaking as the body reacts to high levels of stress.

These are some of the main physical symptoms that may indicate burnout. If you are suffering from any of these symptoms, it is important to consult your GP to verify the cause. These symptoms do not necessarily imply burnout, but may indicate a medical problem.

Fletcher addresses the issue of stress-related illness when he writes:

> Stress can kill. It is responsible for more industrial disease than any other aspect of work. It compromises the immune system, plays a highly important role in the onset of major diseases, and can result in premature death. It also makes people feel anxious and depressed, lowers their job and life satisfaction, makes for bad decisions and poor organisational climate, increases alcohol and cigarette consumption, increases health service costs, leads to accidents, and reduces efficiency. These aspects are only the tip of the iceberg. What is so strange is that employers and governments are largely ignoring the problem and even worry about addressing the issue of stress in case it raises expectations that something will be done about it or, even worse, that the very mention of the word causes people to think about the issues.[13]

Emotional symptoms of burnout

There is a variety of emotional responses to stress:

Emotional exhaustion

Sufferers may find it difficult to 'feel' emotionally. They may wonder if they have grown hard or unloving from their emotional overload, resulting in numbness. Others may react in an opposite way and feel emotional about everything or anything. They may feel that they cannot cope and the smallest problem appears so large that they frequently burst into tears. This condition afflicts men as well as women and men may find themselves extremely close to tears for long periods, or indeed weeping in ways they never have before.

Feelings of dread

This is the feeling that at any moment something awful will happen. It may include fears that a family member may have a terrible accident or that something is about to befall the sufferer: an inexplicable awareness of pending doom.

Fear

This is a broad category. The sufferer may feel the fear of failure or discovery and have a strong sense of vulnerability. Some people fear for their health and worry over every twinge or discomfort. If you are in fear for your health it is better to go to the GP and have your concerns checked. Others fear things like the telephone ringing. They have grown to equate the telephone ring with someone's cry for help and cannot face giving out any more. Irrational fears are common among those suffering from burnout. Sufferers don't necessarily think their fears are irrational; they seem so real to them during these difficult times.

Anger and irritability

Sufferers may develop a 'short fuse' and find themselves easily irritated or angry. To some this is a normal trait, but others develop it uncharacteristically. This may place added strain on any and all of their relationships and exacerbate any relationship difficulties.

Persecution complex

This may link with the above. Sufferers may begin to believe that people are discussing them behind their backs. This often begins as a fantasy but can become a reality as friends, church members and colleagues notice the paranoia and comment on it, either from concern or criticism (particularly where the minister has created a heavy dependency on him among his congregation).

Loss of optimism

Sufferers may have little enthusiasm for anything, and any helpful suggestions made to them may meet with a negative response. This may also be true when sufferers are being encouraged to find a path of recovery from burnout. They may not believe that they will ever feel better than they do in the present and often deny that there is anything wrong.

Loss of courage

Risk-taking may become a serious problem for the sufferer. This is particularly true for those who have been helped on their way to burnout by heavy criticism of their leadership or gifting. Many activities become risks and risks become highly threatening.

Loss of self-esteem

Sufferers of burnout often experience a lowering sense of self-worth and loss of self-respect. They may change their patterns in areas like cleanliness and dress. Sufferers have been known to exhibit alternative behaviour. Smart, clean people have become slovenly, scruffy and unkempt out of an inner belief that they are worthless. They may consider themselves as complete failures and become highly emotional. Some ministers have left the ministry for this reason. Their condition was never diagnosed and they felt that their only recourse was to quit.

Depression

Sufferers from burnout may become increasingly depressed. It is important that people who begin to feel depressed pay a visit to their GP, or indeed that they do so if those close to them consider that they are becoming depressed. Depression takes on many and varied forms. If in doubt, check it out!

Lowered resistance to infection

The sufferer may more easily catch a cold or other illnesses, or become infected in a wound.

Lowered inhibitions

The sufferer may find it easier to give in to temptation while burned out. (I say more about this under 'Spiritual symptoms' below.)

Time-wasting

Sufferers may waste much more time than ever before:

1. They may do a little and consider it to be a lot.
2. They make problems out to be larger than they are.
3. They may invent elaborate schemes to overcome minor problems.
4. They find it difficult to concentrate and may have a shorter attention span.
5. They may make unnecessary telephone calls as an excuse for not working.
6. They may take unnecessary trips.
7. They attempt anything to run away from their work without actually running away.

These are some of the more common emotional symptoms attending the sufferer of burnout. Burnout is a form of emotional exhaustion that is for many a hell on earth. They experience an emotional roller-coaster ride not easily recognised by others. I have worked with Christian ministers whose partners have found it difficult to understand the condition and the dramatic change in personality. Burnout is a disorder that develops gradually, and it is therefore difficult to identify its beginnings.

Spiritual symptoms of burnout

The general downward pull of the condition can easily have that effect on the spiritual life too. What follows is a brief list of some of the more obvious symptoms.

Lack of enthusiasm

There may be a lack of enthusiasm for the spiritual life. The sufferer may relegate the spiritual life to the bottom of the pile of things that are important.

Stepping back

Sufferers from burnout may begin to step back from involvement in spiritual activity. They may pray, preach, teach and attend church much less than before, and may find many reasons why this is in the best interest of the church. Stepping back temporarily from some of these things is probably wise for healing, but not from a position of denial.

Anger at God

Sufferers may have decided that their suffering is undeserved and that

God has somehow failed them. They become angry with Him, but may have difficulty accepting it. Burnout is usually experienced as the result of working and living patterns that have evolved or been chosen by the individual. It results from our own actions and not those of others.

Doubt
Doubting the existence of God is a more or less frequent visitor to every Christian, but sufferers from burnout may experience a profound doubt of God since they feel so unlike their former selves. Their emotional trauma is reflected in their asking, 'How can God exist if I feel so terrible and live in such darkness?' Their spiritual experience suffers in tandem with their bodies and emotions; they feel awful and their thoughts reflect this.

Guilt
Sufferers from burnout may feel a strong sense of guilt. Their condition renders them ineffective, yet they feel guilty for it. Many have believed that Christian ministers are the strong ones, able to bear all things and keep going in the face of adversity. They have often denied their humanity to the point that their humanity is fighting back for survival. They may also feel guilty for the doubts mentioned above.

A desert experience
A spiritual gloom or barrenness, often described as a 'desert experience', may be encountered, in which there would seem to be no oasis of meaning. (Although a desert experience may indeed be a positive aspect of one's spiritual journey, in this instance it is seen as simply dry.)

Pain, either physical or emotional, has been created as a warning to prevent injury or to alert us to some problem within our system. Burnout comes from ignoring the warning for a long time. It is like a railway journey, with the ultimate destination a complete physical and emotional breakdown. Fortunately the train stops at every station and we can disembark before the journey's end.

Reflection

Are you able to identify any of the symptoms of burnout in your own life?

Effects of burnout

Many of the effects of burnout become visible in the consideration of the symptoms.

Common effects of burnout

Withdrawing

A person suffering from burnout may begin to withdraw emotionally. The life of a church leader involves a high level of contact with other people. Often when the minister is suffering high stress or burnout they will withdraw from relationships and fear public appearances. Appearing in role, in public, requires a great deal of emotional energy. A person will often develop a 'persona', or public self. When resources are low, there is insufficient energy left for these presentations of self.

This 'in role' experience becomes much less attractive and can reach a point where it may even become terrifying, and a mild form of paranoia may be experienced. A number of ministers suffering from burnout have been completely shocked by their inner feelings. They are terrified of their role as a minister and cannot come to terms with the fear that the role invokes. Their response is to withdraw.

Avoiding

Burnout sufferers may begin to avoid their role. Burnout is not simply switched on overnight; it builds like a small flame, eventually turning into a forest fire. Ministers may avoid aspects of their work, and this process may begin almost imperceptibly. They may join more committees, read more books, attend more conferences. They are finding a semi-legitimate means of escaping the role causing their pain and stress. It requires a high degree of self-awareness here for a person to perceive their own avoidance.

Becoming less approachable

The role of the minister is largely person-centred, as it involves working with people. Not only may ministers withdraw, but their manner may also be such that they become less approachable. They may become irritable as a result of anger welling up inside. People will begin to avoid them, as they feel uncomfortable. This is difficult for ministers, since they will be less able to engage in self-analysis and evaluate the problem.

Family problems
A person suffering from burnout may develop serious family problems. Sufferers lose the ability to monitor or control their emotional changes. They are less sensitive to and less aware of others. They may become the centre of their own universe, feeling so bad that they cannot escape their own needs in favour of others. This may make them difficult to live with and cause embarrassment, since their behaviour may not be limited to the privacy of the home. This has serious consequences on family life. One's partner and children may misinterpret the signs and feel unwanted and unloved.

Openness to sin
One of the most destructive effects of burnout is the increased susceptibility to sin. Temptations long held at bay seem to take on new strength and the sufferer may have much less resistance to them. Old sinful patterns may return and new ones may develop. Many people suffer from serious sexual temptation as they endeavour to comfort their pain. They equate sexual pleasure with love and comfort and are unable to resist the allure of eroticism. Others are no longer able to handle the relational aspects of their marriage and want 'gratification without complication'.

Gratification replaces mutual loving and many succumb to pornography. Some ministers have had to cancel their Internet subscription and come off-line, because they are no longer able to trust themselves with the instant availability of pornography. Some sufferers enter into sexual affairs as a means of feeding the emotional vacuum. Other sufferers from burnout have used an emotional or sexual affair as a means of leaving the ministry – they have found it easier to choose what may be considered as the emergence of an obvious enemy rather than face their deepest inner needs.

As mentioned earlier in the book, Schaumburg describes a condition that he calls 'sexual addiction', which is a state of mind connected with the fear of intimacy. It suggests that a person may adopt a behavioural pattern that allows them to look for sexual gratification outside an intimate personal relationship. This is sought not merely as the answer to a moment's need, but as a life pattern that moves people further away from the intimate, personal, loving relationship they desire. The more they pursue false intimacy, the less chance of real intimacy.[14] It is possible to reach a place, through stress and burnout, where sexual activity is seriously negatively affected.

Loss of productivity
A person suffering from burnout will begin to be less productive. Christian ministers will almost certainly become more ineffective in what they do. Their gifts and abilities are numbed by their emotional condition and they cannot produce at the same rate as previously. Often sufferers will grind to a complete halt in what they can do.

Wanting to give up
A person suffering from burnout may want to give up their ministry. Our research here has shown that 28 per cent of all Protestant ministers are considering giving up the ministry at any point in time. This is far more serious than 'feeling low' about your role. The rate of fall-out of ministers across the Church in the UK is alarming. One denomination (which wishes to remain nameless) lost 203 ministers in a three-year period, 93 of whom never returned to the ministry. Some ministers not only leave their calling, but also leave the Church completely as a result of undiagnosed and untreated burnout.

For all of these reasons, burnout is a serious condition. It is destructive, wasteful and no respecter of persons. This destructive force can be stopped and, with a sensitive approach, can be avoided. A system of survival or an avoidance strategy needs to be employed to overcome the effects of burnout and to prevent it from taking place at all.

Reflection

Are you able to identify any of the effects of burnout in your own life?

The following two worksheets will help you to measure whether you are close to being burned out.

WORKSHEET 1

Are You Burned Out?

Materials are from *Burnout in the Ministry* by Brooks R. Faulkner (Nashville: Broadman Press, 1981).

For each statement, circle whether this is rarely true (R) in your life, sometimes true (S) or usually true (U).

R	S	U	
0	1	2	I feel exhausted and run down
0	1	2	I am irritable
0	1	2	I get frustrated easily
0	1	2	I feel helpless
0	1	2	I have trouble sleeping
0	1	2	I am discouraged
0	1	2	I tend to be critical of others
0	1	2	I tend to be critical of myself
0	1	2	I want to get away from people
0	1	2	I would like to change my job
0	1	2	I feel spiritually dull
0	1	2	I think that my job is stressful
0	1	2	I feel under constant pressure
0	1	2	I have difficulty being with troubled people
0	1	2	I am impatient
0	1	2	I lack enthusiasm

(If you scored 16–32 points, you may be a victim of burnout.)

WORKSHEET 2

Burnout Worksheet

Materials are from *Burnout* by Myron Rush (Chariot Victor Publishing, 1987). Used by permission.

This is not a test; it's a worksheet to help you determine if you have symptoms of burnout. For each statement choose a score ranging from 1 to 5, based on how closely you agree with the statement. A score of 1 means a very definite no, and a 5 means a very definite yes. Consider the past six months when giving your answer.

1. I seem to be working harder but accomplishing less 1 2 3 4 5
2. I dread going to work each day 1 2 3 4 5
3. I seem to have less physical energy than before 1 2 3 4 5
4. Things irritate me that in the past didn't bother me 1 2 3 4 5
5. More and more I find myself trying to avoid people 1 2 3 4 5
6. I seem to be getting more short tempered 1 2 3 4 5
7. I am having a harder time concentrating 1 2 3 4 5
8. More and more I find myself not wanting to get out of bed in the morning 1 2 3 4 5
9. I am starting to lose confidence in my abilities 1 2 3 4 5
10. I am finding it harder and harder to concentrate on my work 1 2 3 4 5
11. It is getting harder for me to take risks 1 2 3 4 5
12. I am becoming more dissatisfied with my accomplishments 1 2 3 4 5
13. Lately I have started blaming God for my situation 1 2 3 4 5
14. Some days I just want to run away from everything 1 2 3 4 5
15. I care less and less if my work ever gets done or not 1 2 3 4 5
16. It seems that everything is staying the same or getting worse 1 2 3 4 5
17. It seems that everything I try to do takes more energy than I have 1 2 3 4 5
18. I am finding it hard to do even simple and routine tasks 1 2 3 4 5
19. I wish people would just leave me alone 1 2 3 4 5
20. I am frustrated with the changes I see in myself 1 2 3 4 5

Scoring Your Burnout Worksheet:

0–30 points = You are in no danger of burnout
31–45 points = You are developing some of the symptoms of burnout
46–60 points = You are probably starting to burn out
61–75 points = You are definitely in the burnout process
Over 75 points = You are in the advanced stages of burnout

This burnout worksheet is designed to give you some general guidelines for determining burnout. It is not a burnout test. After taking this inventory, if you feel you may have some of the symptoms of burnout, discuss it with a counsellor. (If you are unable to find a counsellor then contact the Claybury Trust (020 8906 2737) for further help.)

I would encourage anyone reading this book to continue their journey by reading more widely on the subjects of stress and burnout to further enable an informed and healthy approach to their ministry lives.

10. Overcoming Ministry Burnout

In this chapter you will be able to build on your understanding of burnout from the last chapter and consider skills and tools that are available. You will learn how to avoid burnout and how to overcome it for yourself and others. Your awareness of stress management will be increased.

Overcoming anything requires a personal commitment to a direction and this subject is no different, except for the fact that the depressive nature of burnout makes it that much harder to take the medicine, good though it may be. I experienced burnout some eight years after starting out in the ministry. I didn't see it coming and didn't know that it was there when I was experiencing it; I just knew that I could no longer cope with things as they were. For me, the long learning curve of recovery became not only my healer but my teacher too. I learned what was wrong with me as I began to recover. It is my hope that you may be prevented from sharing my experience through reading this book and applying its lessons to your ministry and life. I also hope that any readers who are currently experiencing burnout may find help here for their recovery.

The high incidence of stress

I have shown that burnout is a result of being overstressed for a prolonged period. Our research and my working experience with leaders has suggested that Christian ministers working under stressful conditions, with high expectations for long periods, are prone to the condition of burnout. In this chapter we will look at handling burnout along the continuum from prevention to cure. The result will be a suggested therapeutic strategy to maintain health in ministry.

So far, I have shown that the Christian ministry is a response to a call or sense of 'vocation'. This call sets the role apart from other caring professions since it includes a sense of the voice of God. Following a calling is a different dynamic, then, and Coate illustrates this well when discussing the 'strain' of relating to God that ministers may face as public faith holders or representatives of belief. She writes:

> In facing this dilemma ministers are in a quite different position to other caring professionals whose role on the whole stops short of explicit exposure and explication of their ultimate belief position. Any professional has values, and it is naive to think that they do not affect his or her work, but usually there is elbow-room for development, doubt modification and negation. But Christian ministers are committed to the Christian faith, Jewish rabbis to the Jewish faith; furthermore, both are committed to expounding and teaching these very traditions.[1]

Christian ministers carry out a public role that can be highly stressful, and may find themselves endeavouring to carry out a heavy workload with few resources to sustain it. Fletcher, when discussing research undertaken that included a review of clergy workload, writes:

> Workloads for a substantial proportion of them were quite high. Over one-fifth took more than three services on an average Sunday, and 13 per cent were responsible for more than three places of worship. A quarter took eleven or more occasional offices per month, over half had no secretarial help at all for parish affairs, and there was considerable use of the parsonage household (which for some caused considerable difficulties). Over one-third of the clergy wives were in paid employment, although it was also clear that many wives were significant helpers in parish matters and provided the married clergy with considerable support in their work. Forty-five per cent of the clergy were at least 'frequently' rushed off their feet, with a similar number reporting significant role ambiguities. Conflicts of role in the job were also commonplace.[2]

Burnout, then, is the using up or wasting of inner resources through working until there is nothing left to give. This state of having nothing left can be frightening to sufferers, who may be used to shaping their own destiny. Such people have been driven by inner motivational forces to arrive at this burnt-out state. Suddenly, the driveshaft is broken, and nothing will work in quite the same way. They find themselves in a world that is unfamiliar and threatening, lost in another dimension with no way out.

The following text looks at the 'prevention to cure' continuum and offers practical steps for avoiding and overcoming burnout.

In the last chapter I gave burnout the following description: 'The exhausting of the inner resource that enables a carer to go on caring. The using up of the essential "inner you", rendering the individual in a serious condition of disfunctionality. The spending of self on others in such a way that the "inner bank balance" has gone into the red.'

This chapter will include discussion in the following areas:

- Immediate responses to burnout
- Confronting the causes
- Modifying behaviour
- Skill improvement
- The future

As we begin to look at this subject it is important to note at the outset that recovery from burnout is gradual and often slow. Generally people are looking for immediate results from the treatments outlined below, but these are few. Those around us may also be expecting a fairly fast recovery and may not understand the time it may take to effect even a partial recovery.

Case study

Ben is a Free Church minister. He had been serving for eight years as a pastoral elder in a church. His position in the church had not been clearly defined and he spent years attempting to work out his role. Little that Ben did seemed to meet with the approval of the church – it was as if they were all working to a different set of expectations of him.

He had grown up in a family where his older brother was constantly praised for his achievements. Ben always felt that he was living in his brother's shadow and worked all the harder to achieve the same level of praise, but without success.

Ben had developed a low self-esteem and adopted a pattern of working that he had hoped would make him feel better about himself and earn him some much needed praise. It didn't matter how well Ben did, for it was never enough to please him or to lift his self-esteem. Ben was a classic case for burnout and after eight years of service in this church he found himself severely stressed. His stresses would surface in tears and feelings of dread. He began to believe that others were talking about him negatively and that his family was against him. He gradually developed a mild paranoia over this and reached a point where he could no longer work and was in danger of major physical and emotional collapse.

I spent time with Ben and diagnosed a case of burnout, subsequently confirmed by a GP. Ben entered into a three-month plan of action that included stopping work, and receiving supportive therapy in the USA. This was designed to bring him to the beginning of his recovery. Ben's church had helped finance his recovery programme and, regardless of information to the contrary, had formed the opinion that after three months he would be well again. Ben returned from his 'time out' feeling much better for his supported break and went back to his old way of working. Nothing had changed in terms of his own or his church's expectations. Within a month Ben went into emotional collapse and experienced what he described as his 'living hell'. He was in a worse condition than at the point of diagnosis. He and his church had expected too much too soon. Too little had been done in the healing process and Ben was in a serious condition. The church didn't know what to make of it and eventually asked Ben to resign, which felt like a hammer blow to a man who had no idea why he felt as he did.

It is a mistake to expect recovery to take place quickly. The dynamics that cause burnout have to be understood and methodically worked through for a measured and paced recovery to take place. After three years of supportive therapy, Ben is showing signs not only of having recovered but also of having changed his life completely. He is now equipped to live and work in a way that will keep him from any future burnout. Ben is a new man and working well as a senior pastor in another church.

Immediate responses to burnout

There are a number of immediate responses that need to be made to help the sufferer recover.

Removal from the heat

Like the victim of a terrible fire, the sufferer must be removed immediately from the flames and smoke. The longer they remain exposed to danger, the worse the nature of the injury. This sounds simple but the heat here is not so easily recognised as in an actual fire. The sufferer from burnout may behave like someone desperate to get back into the fire, without realising the danger, and needs to be held back by others.

Stop working

Burnout sufferers must be strongly encouraged to stop working. This is not to say that they will do no work throughout their recovery but, as a first-aid response, they must stop working and recognise the severity of their condition. Since burnout is little understood, this first-aid response is not always easy to achieve. McBurney writes:

> The treatment of burnout is fourfold. First, the person must be allowed to rest. Removal from responsibility is essential, since a significant part of the syndrome is fatigue. A supportive environment is important where love and acceptance are available.[3]

Some employers (including churches) have difficulty with this and are reluctant to allow their employees the necessary sick leave. It is important that sufferers see their GP and have their condition ratified by the medical services. Doctors will often prescribe a period of leave of absence, since they recognise the need to be free from responsibilities.

Supportive environment

Stopping work may seem like entering a vacuum. It is important that 'stopping' has some structure to it and that some necessary elements are in place.

- The sufferer must not be left alone to recover.
- The individual concerned needs to have people around who are sensitive and understanding.
- The sufferer should not be exposed to people who represent the same field of responsibility, such as church members or leaders. These people remind the sufferer of work by their conversation and proximity.
- The people surrounding the sufferer must be supportive, caring and loving and should not crowd the individual but allow space punctuated by intervals of togetherness.
- Family members and others need to reassure the sufferer that they are

still respected and loved. This will stop the intense feeling of failure and inferiority that accompanies this condition.

- Sufferers should be loved, even when they are abrasive and angry.
- Sufferers should know that it is OK if they feel like screaming and shouting. They should be allowed to express these emotions.
- Sufferers should not be put under pressure or made to work to another person's schedule.
- Helpers should not attempt to be counsellors. This will confuse the roles that each helper will play. The sufferer needs loving support as well as a counsellor. These are different roles.

Rest and relaxation

The sufferer will need to rest and relax at this time. This is not easy since the sufferer is emerging from a time of intense activity. Many people who are suffering from burnout have lost the art of rest; they do not know what to do with their time out.

- Time spent resting needs to have a gentle structure to it. Sufferers will need help to establish how best to use their time.
- It is often helpful if the sufferer and the family can get away from the area for a time. The change of scenery and the stimulation of different surroundings can facilitate recovery.
- The sufferer does not need to be exposed to the problems of the world during this stage. Watching television and reading newspapers may appear to be relaxing, but the sufferer may begin to worry about the state of the world.
- Peace and quiet may be helpful to sufferers, in which case they should be encouraged to avoid loud music, crowds and noisy places.
- Sleep is vital, as patterns of sleep may have become distorted by stress. Sufferers must be allowed to develop a natural pattern of sleep, without feeling guilty of laziness. They must be encouraged to get the rest that they need. A natural sleep pattern will take time to develop as the adrenaline levels subside. The body will eventually relax instead of preparing for battle and a normal sleep pattern will emerge. The number of hours of sleep needs to be recorded to establish a better sleeping pattern when the sufferer has recovered. Ideally sleep will be natural, though a doctor may prescribe medication to kick-start the process. Either way, alarm clocks should be avoided.

Case study

Jean and Bob were deeply committed to their calling in the Methodist ministry. They saw it as a joint ministry even though Bob was the recognised minister. They had attempted to be careful about time off and relationships and had been taking their day off each week, but somehow they seemed to spend it shopping or fulfilling some other domestic chore. The day was often interrupted anyway and it was financially difficult to take quality time out.

A good friend of Jean and Bob's had noticed that they were hard at work over many months without a decent break. He felt that something should be done and arranged to have money made available to them for a night out together. It wasn't a huge sum but enough for them to choose to do one thing that evening. Jean and Bob looked forward to their night out and worked harder to clear their responsibilities so that nothing would interfere.

The night came and Jean and Bob felt quite exhausted, but they dressed in their best for a night to remember. Jean spent extra time dressing because she didn't quite know what to wear; it had been so long since she had had a night out! Once ready they said goodnight to the baby-sitter and got into the car parked at the front gate. Bob started the engine and froze. Jean looked at him wondering whatever was the matter. Bob said to her, 'Where are we going?' Jean looked blank and panicked because she could not answer the question. A sudden realisation gripped them both: they had forgotten how to arrange an outing, and couldn't remember how to relax and enjoy themselves!

This is a true story with only the names changed. It may not seem to be too serious, but it illustrates how easily work may become the central focus of our lives and we may lose the art of rest and relaxation.

Professional help

A contributory factor to burnout is the secrecy or isolation experienced by the individual. It is common that sufferers may never have seen a counsellor for themselves even though they have counselled others or referred many for counselling. It is important that sufferers from burnout be gently but firmly encouraged to get professional help at this time.

The doctor

The medical needs of the individual are important. It is common for burnout sufferers to experience a range of health problems, such as muscle pain, high blood pressure, lowered resistance to infection, headaches, diarrhoea, etc. It is good for sufferers to build relationships with their GP, who can help them recover. Some of the physical symptoms experienced are similar to those experienced in major illnesses such as cancer and heart disease, which can be highly alarming. Sufferers may experience a sense of impending doom and be absolutely sure that they are about to die or have a mental breakdown.

The counsellor/psychologist

Sufferers from burnout must establish relationships with their counsellors or psychologists. They need the support of these professionals to be able to work through the issues and make a healthy recovery.

Resistance

It is common for sufferers to resist professional help towards recovery for two reasons:

1. They are not familiar with the role switch from helper to the helped. Caring for others has become integral to their perception of themselves, to their very identity.
2. They may attack any schedule of recovery with the same spirit of critical perfectionism that has become a norm in their driven lives.

Denial

Sufferers have been denying their need to themselves and others until it has become a practised art. Since they have now reached the position of advanced and debilitating stress, they can no longer keep going, but they may still deny the serious nature of their condition. Many force themselves back to work believing that they can shrug off their condition in the same way that they have before. 'If I just keep working then I will be OK', they may say. A counsellor will be able to help them to admit that they need help and that they are not failing because of this. Often they have subconsciously believed that they are superhuman and different from their flock.

Insecurity
A professional is essential since sufferers have a low level of trust of others in terms of self-disclosure. Many Christian ministers have been living on their persona and have kept their real feelings to themselves. They have been wounded in the past and are reluctant to reveal to anyone the truth about their inner person for fear of being discovered as a fraud or a weaker person than they are perceived to be. Burnout sufferers are unlikely to talk about their deepest feelings and issues without trusting their counsellor completely.

Professionals
Sufferers need to feel safe and in the hands of someone who will understand them. They often feel isolated. Counsel will be received mostly from psychologists or experienced professional counsellors, particularly where these professionals have a sound awareness of Christian leadership issues. The need to be understood is high here. Other Christian ministers who are qualified as counsellors are helpful, because they are seen as streetwise. They are colleagues who know at first hand what the sufferers have experienced.

Reflection

How does this statement make you feel: 'Christian ministers may attack any schedule of recovery with the same spirit of critical perfectionism that has become a norm in their driven lives'?

Support group
Sufferers from burnout experience many emotional feelings – isolation and abnormality among them. They feel stigmatised and sense that they have lost their place, having fallen behind in their work. They are concerned about others finding out.

It is important to establish a support group that is available to sufferers should they reach out to others.

Family members
This must include close family, particularly the spouse, and may include close and trusted friends.

Trusted colleagues

These may also be a part of a support group, if they represent no threat to the sufferer. Anyone involved in the support group must avoid talking about work and responsibility. Peer pressure may have been an aspect of the minister's life that contributed to the state of burnout. Coate writes:

> Other dioceses and bodies have provided the possibility of peer support from an early stage in ministry, most often in groups. They are making the point, often building on some aspects of, for example, theological college life, that sharing can be an integral and natural part of ministry. But being personally open in a group can seem rather threatening, for peer pressure sometimes feels even *worse than that of authority*.[4]

The members of the group must not be tempted to offer advice and cross the line into counselling, which may confuse sufferers and make it difficult for them to work with their professional. The group must respect the need for confidentiality in these circumstances and the sufferer must not overhear them discussing the situation. The support group must be prepared to be in place for a long period of time. It is not uncommon for sufferers to remain in a critical condition for as long as eighteen months after they have begun their recovery programme, and to take several years to regain a place of health.

The aim behind this approach to burnout is to allow the minister the space to recognise what has happened and to facilitate a process of recovery. I have found that a number of my clients who are suffering burnout knew that their lives were severely strained, but made no attempt to evaluate their circumstances until they were stopped by major stress and accompanying health warnings like palpitations of the heart, or pain. Almost one-fifth of ministers who felt overworked (in our research) were planning to take no action to resolve the situation. Sometimes a serious condition like burnout is the experience that finally gets the minister's attention, since the warning signs have been ignored. Ministers, and particularly those already suffering burnout, need the space to re-evaluate the nature of their working lives. An educative process needs to be experienced to inform the ministers and facilitate their awareness of their own emotional and spiritual issues. Burnout is enormously wasteful both in terms of the life of ministers and the life of the church they serve.

Confronting the causes

The processes that cause burnout need to be examined, understood and defused in a person's life in order for health to return.

Low self-worth

Those who suffer from burnout often have a low self-worth. They have been driven to the point of near collapse and are no longer able to work at their usual rate. They are also unable to see their usual results. They feel like failures and were feeling this way for some time before they were forced to stop working.

Examine the drivenness

Sufferers may have been driven by a deep-rooted need to gain parental approval or to earn the love and respect they have felt lacking in their lives. Whatever the reason, all burnout victims have had unhealthy patterns of work. They have been driven by inner forces to do more than any human being should. This drive needs to be examined with the sufferer (preferably by the counsellor or psychologist) in order that it can be re-evaluated.

True worth found in God

The sufferer needs to learn that his or her worth is found in God and not in results. The Western world is very much results-oriented: produce the goods or you are out. Many executives have found themselves on the professional scrap heap at an early age for non-acceptable production levels. Non-invasive spiritual renewal may be possible – that is, a quiet prayer with a friend – but only where the feelings of guilt and failure can be avoided. Facing God as welcoming Father is difficult when one feels like a failed son or daughter.

Grace of God

Burnout sufferers often have no understanding of the grace of God and tend to focus on work and results. They have taken their encouragement from achievement and not from God's unconditional love. They need to be reminded gently of the grace of God.

Lack of encouragement

Sufferers may have gone for long periods with little feedback and need to be affirmed and encouraged. This can be a difficult task since they may have developed an entrenched belief in their own worthlessness.

Recall

It may be helpful to recall places and people that have been positively affected by the ministry of the individual concerned. Avoid pointing to achievements that were a part of the burnout process.

Encouragement

Sufferers may be helped by listing their particular gifts and strengths. Encourage with truth only. The temptation to help someone by stretching the truth is strong but damaging, and the sufferer will eventually see through it anyway.

Tokens

Show your love for sufferers with acts of kindness. Many Christian ministers cannot afford to go out to a restaurant, buy music or a beautiful book or go to the cinema. This is a good time to give love tokens to sufferers, who will respond well to this tangible love. Remember not to send them anywhere alone. Let them go as a couple if they are married or go with a good friend if they are single. Don't let them view this as therapy but love.

Ghosts

The sufferer from burnout may be troubled by memories of past failures or misunderstandings. These 'ghosts' have a wearing effect and can be part of the cause of the drivenness that has led the sufferer to burnout. They need to be exorcised.

Parents

Sometimes problems with their parents may have left unresolved tensions. It can be a good plan to get sufferers to meet with their parents to discuss their feelings with them.

Situations

Sufferers may recall unhappy situations. It can be a good plan to have them meet again with people who were involved and have a much more positive view put of how things went and how the sufferer handled the situation. But avoid doing this where you are not sure of the dynamics.

Laying to rest

Sufferers may have a number of haunting and stressful memories that can be laid to rest by gentle and skilful reappraisal. Many memories are distorted by time and fantasy. Helping sufferers to see that these memor-ies are fantasies and not condemning truths can be powerful in defusing them.

Value system

Sufferers from burnout may have developed a value system that is deeply embedded and based on 'success'. In the Western world the worship of success causes people in different professions to push themselves and others to perform to inhuman levels.

Being seen and heard

Personal ambition exists within the Church. Few will call it by its name, but many church leaders are driven by ambition. Being acknowledged by well-known speakers is definitely the desire of many, and becoming a well-known speaker is the desire of even more. A fine line exists between being successful for God and being successful for self. Many are working with the latter while believing it is the former. This ambitious appetite is never fulfilled. It causes individuals to work too hard for their cause. Few will say no when they should if they are asked to perform a task that may earn them some kudos.

Bigger churches

Many Christian ministers secretly desire to lead larger and more prestigious churches. Success is understood here as greater numbers and size. This view suggests that bigger churches are better churches. It also courts the thought that the bigger the church you lead the more effective you are. This is a terrible trap for ministers. They tend towards counting the congregation or at least making a mental note of the spaces in the sanctuary. Their own success is then based on how many people attend the services. It is a form of identifying with the congregation. There are serious problems with this view:

- It drives individuals to become actors instead of normal human beings as they attempt to become more attractive in their role to enhance the attendance figures.
- It makes leaders of smaller churches believe that they are inadequate.
- It ignores other church growth dynamics that may exist.

Being and doing

A healthy value system is based on self-awareness and God-awareness. Concentration on your being helps you to realise that you are one of God's children, part of the household of God, because of the work of Jesus on the cross and not because of the product of your labours. From this basis of security in God, we are more able to adopt a healthy working pattern. Healthy doing comes best from healthy being. Doers who are out of balance are looking for importance based on what they do and, as a result, on what they may become. This is an unhealthy value system that drives individuals and is liable to cause burnout.

Case study

Ben, from earlier in this chapter, had focused heavily on being a success. He had courted relationships with 'well-known' Christian leaders and had analysed their lifestyles. Ben's analysis was not accurate and he had focused on his own imagined ideas about these characters. He then began to emulate his heroes with the disastrous results that I mentioned earlier. Ben was also being driven by a desire to be a 'big name'. He felt that he would only be successful in his own eyes and the eyes of others if he could make it, and reach the big time. He had lost touch with reality and with his spirituality. He was driven to perform impossible tasks.

The value system of ministers may be an important determining factor as to whether they will ever burn out. The more people are 'driven' to succeed the more they are likely to burn out.

Reflection

What feelings does this statement produce in you: 'A fine line exists between being successful for God and being successful for self. Many are working with the latter while believing it is the former'?

Personality type

A number of indicators suggest that human beings have different personality types and that most human beings fall within one or two of these types. While there are different views and philosophies about this, the evidence tends to suggest that this is largely true. The more we learn about ourselves the more we are likely to be in touch with the things that stress and concern us. This awareness can be a helpful tool in avoidance of, and recovery from, burnout.

Modifying behaviour

The avoidance of burnout is an issue closely bound up with overall personal health. The initiatives to be taken for a healthy church are the responsibility of three related groups: the denomination (where one exists), the congregation, and the individual minister. These three groups must co-operate if realistic expectations and working boundaries are to be established to avoid the overstress of the profession of Christian ministry.

Each of the above three groups needs to become aware of the findings of research to educate themselves into the professional stressors of the Christian ministry. Coate writes:

> Alleviation of strain will depend on trying to understand its causes as fully as we can; otherwise we shall bypass the real problem and the stress and strain are likely to build up again when the impact and impetus of first-aid measures has faded.[5]

An educational process needs to be entered into if the Church is going to see a change in the 28 per cent of clergy who may leave their role in the Church. Coate argues:

> Among the most likely effects of stress are illness, either life-threatening or chronically debilitating, dependence on alcohol or other drugs, personal emotional breakdown, marital breakdown in those religious tradi-

> tions in which marriage is allowed and difficulties with celibacy in those where it is not. There may also be an external move out of ministry or a more internal move away from any sense of vocation.[6]

Increased levels of self-awareness on the part of the Christian minister would be a great advantage. One of the issues for the minister here is a failure to recognise self-awareness as distinct from selfishness. This self-awareness would serve best if the information that it produced led to a commitment to behavioural changes. Behavioural changes may be those that we make regarding things that we do or things that we may begin to include that are new ministry motifs.

Ministry motif

Reviews

Professional reviews can be helpful tools in the quest for healthy awareness. A review is a system of measuring whether the expectations of both the church and the minister are being met. A level of fear and dislike for this activity exists because of the wide experience of reviews in a competitive society. But reviews can be seen as positive tools if they enable both the church members and the minister helpfully to oversee the running of the congregation.

Supervisory systems

The role of Christian minister is one of the few professional caring roles that does not often involve formal supervision sessions. Coate, when referring to one of her case studies, writes:

> John and those in similar positions are often seen as having an enviable degree of autonomy in their work, as compared to other professionals. But this very freedom can involve a blurring of the lines of accountability and responsibility, and so become, in itself, a source of strain.[7]

This autonomy, while it may seem freeing and desirable, lacks an element of supervision that could be an oversight in two areas:

1. Ministers are not processing their interface and skill in ministry with a significant trusted other in a relationship that helps to hone and shape skills.

2. Ministers are not being held accountable for safe practice with their clients and this puts both client and minister at risk.

Formal supervision sessions, then, can prove to be a support system for the ministry.

Denominational support

This is an important area that has at its heart some essential hurdles to be overcome before it can be the positive support that it seeks and needs to be. Research supports the view that many serving ministers are not comfortable with the levels of confidentiality that they have either experienced or believe to exist. Fletcher writes, regarding denominational support: 'In general, the bishop/archdeacon/rural dean was perceived to be largely irrelevant to work matters by about one-third of clergy, although a significant minority of 14 per cent found them supportive.'[8]

From my client-base, many of the ministers not using their 'line managers' as a source of support are not doing so because they fear that confidentiality may not be upheld and that their future may be affected by any disclosures that they would make. An element of mistrust needs to be overcome for this to function at its best. I am very much aware that in a number of cases denominations have formed confidential, professional counselling and support services that are excellent and can be used with confidence.

Spiritual direction

Often misunderstood because it actually refers to a non-directive friend or colleague who guides ministers in their spiritual disciplines. This area of support allows ministers to explore their own spirituality and maintain their own spiritual journey, using the director as facilitator. Mentoring is another way of describing the process of spiritual direction. This is a relationship of safety, one with another, where the mentor is able to offer non-directive help and advice. This is another helpful support system to be encouraged, dependent on the frailty of the protégé who will enter into this mentor–protégé relationship. Power and authority are difficult issues when a minister feels a level of vulnerability. Care needs to be taken when choosing a mentor, but this is a helpful source of ministry support.

The nature of the Christian ministry is such that the minister will often require support and this is a positive strategy for those who want to remain healthy and safe in all their practices. Pre-ordination training could (and occasionally does) include an introduction to these forms of support.

Modifying behaviour means changing the way we live when we have discovered that some of our life habits are not helpful. If we consider that some of the patterns of behaviour are leading us or have led us into burnout, then for our own health's sake we need to change those patterns. What follows simply builds on all that has gone before in this chapter.

Personal motif

Control

Sufferers from burnout have been finding it difficult to release themselves from the mode of 'doing' that they have developed. They have generally developed a heavy regime of work that allows few others to help them. They have taken control and have held on to it. Sufferers need to learn to relinquish control in certain areas of their working life and to delegate.

Trust

Similarly, sufferers need to learn to trust other people with some of their work. Often burnout victims are perfectionists and want everything done to a high standard, sometimes higher than required. Typically these people find the standards of others difficult to accept and therefore rarely delegate. The recovering person needs to learn to relax and let others help. Perfectionism can be adjusted as individuals discover what drives them and are enabled to work on it.

Fears and fantasies

Sufferers need to be encouraged to re-evaluate their fears and fantasies, for these are often the same. We may become afraid of something unreal that takes on major proportions and threatens our health. Perhaps an example of this is the paranoia, common with burnout, that believes that someone is talking about us behind our back. It may be believed, even though it is not true. Before long we may think that everyone is talking about us and that what they have to say is always negative. Sufferers can be helped to face their fears and discover that they are based in fantasy. In this way recoverers can be taught to become the slayers of their own giants.

Regular support

Earlier in this chapter I suggested that a support group be put in place as first aid for the burnout victim. The institution of a regular support group can become a helpful new feature of life and groups of ministers can also meet for honest support of one another.

Openness

Sufferers can be encouraged to adopt a more open approach to their inner feelings for future health. This is not to suggest that they discuss their innermost secrets with everyone – only with trusted and selected others. Perhaps more specifically, sufferers can be encouraged to be more honest with themselves and develop the skills needed for a healthy self-awareness.

Shifting views

Sufferers of burnout have often held rigid views about life, God and themselves. These views are often founded in the stress and strain of life rather than in good thinking and practice. They may be encouraged to rethink and relax some of their hard and fast views and practices.

Slow down

Burnout victims have been living life at a tremendous rate. They walk, talk and eat fast. They often make rushed decisions and are always in a hurry. They pace the floor in social settings and by sheer force of will attempt to get the post delivered more quickly and more often. They are the Grand Prix drivers of the Christian ministry. Such people need to be encouraged to slow down, as it is possible to choose to slow down. Ask family members to comment on the speed at which you eat. Choose the longest queue at the supermarket and relax while you wait. Deliberately walk and talk more slowly. Check yourself regularly and develop different patterns.

Exercise plan

Sufferers from burnout should be encouraged to begin a programme of physical exercise. Professionals agree that physical exercise is one of the foremost stress beaters. The burnout sufferer may have reached such poor physical condition that the advice of a GP and/or professional fitness coach needs to be sought. This programme needs to become a regular feature in the life of the minister.

Spiritual life

Sufferers from burnout often have poor patterns in their spiritual lives. Commonly they have set and reset plans for a better life but have built in a sense of failure, as their speeded up lives will not allow high-quality spiritual devotion. The burnout victim needs to be encouraged with a non-intrusive return to God. God must become a trusted friend again and not an angry parent, employer or headmaster. This is an important aspect of the return to ministry. Sufferers need to feel that they can trust God and also that God can trust them.

Goal-setting

Typically, burnout victims have been helped to their condition by unrealistic goal-setting. They have built in failure by expecting too much of themselves and of everyone else. Often a burnout victim may be surrounded by others who are burned out too, and realistic goal setting must be encouraged by all those around the recovering victim. This may require the help of the support group as the sufferer has no real point of reference for what is realistic. The burnout sufferer has to unlearn and relearn as part of the healing process.

Boundary setting

Sufferers from burnout have been helped towards this critical condition by failing to set realistic boundaries. Time has no meaning for some and they make double bookings in their diaries. They make appointments and are not realistic about the time required to fulfil them. They allow themselves to be contacted by anyone, at any time, regardless of the inconvenience of the interruption. Family times are ruined and study periods interrupted. Setting limits around work could alleviate some stress factors. Hart argues:

> To avoid the stress that results from such a continual state of alertness, a clear message must be sent to the body at the end of every day that it can relax and begin the process of rest and recovery. But how do pastors do this? How do they ascertain that a reasonable day's work has been done? Since the work of pastoring contains no clear inherent boundaries it is usually necessary to create boundaries and to courageously apply them.[9]

Learning to reset realistic boundaries around work and family is an essential process – boundaries like the number of hours one should work each week or how many evenings each week should be reserved for family and leisure. This may involve a wider grasp of the skills of time and project management. The ability to know how much to do within what time frame, and with whom, is essential to healthy ministry. It is impractical to assume that pre-ordination training can offer everything that may be helpful for ministry life within the academic periods of a three- or four-year course, but once again training in setting healthy boundaries in the ministry is advisable.

Such boundaries around life become the 'walls of freedom'. While they draw a line around positive and negative behaviour, they allow life to be lived with a degree of good planning.

To facilitate the setting of healthy ministry boundaries it is important for good levels of communication to ensue between the local church and the minister, the denomination and the minister, and the denomination and the local church. These three elements are significant here in the discussion regarding role and role-delineation. Fletcher argues that

> role ambiguity refers to the person not having a clear enough idea about their role or the job they are doing. It can be due to such factors as uncertain lines of authority, lack of an adequate job description, lack of feedback or the 'fuzzy' boundaries of the job.[10]

These 'fuzzy' boundaries can lead to an imbalanced approach to the work of the ministry and ultimately to negative stress. The suggestion here, then, is that the work of communication of role and role expectations is essential. The denomination and the local congregation need to know and communicate to ministers what their role is and what they expect from it. This would also have to do with the number of hours thought reasonable for ministers to work. As I make this suggestion I am aware that a congregation's expectation of their minister can be so vast that it may be impossible for one person to undertake it.

Communication regarding role and expectations needs to be both informed and realistic. Fletcher writes:

> People can have different expectations concerning their role compared to what others expect of them. Classically, role conflict occurs where an individual is asked to do things which are in conflict with some other job

> function, or where the role they are asked to perform is at odds with what they believe, or with some other role they should fulfil.[11]

Clear lines of communication, where the parties are listening to each other, are necessary for this ideal to be realised.

Humour
Sufferers feel low and depressed. They have not found much to laugh at for a long time, and many have forgotten why they ever laughed before. Involve humour in the life of the recovering victim. Rent funny videos, tell them jokes. Laughter heals.

Fun
Those suffering from burnout have not found fun in their lives for some time. It is important that the recoverers are exposed to fun for fun's sake. Time has had to be used for producing, not wasting. These people need to see again the extravagant nature of God and enjoy life for life's sake.

Case study

Steve had been through the hell of burnout and was taking therapy to help him get over it. The therapist prescribed, 'Go to the theme park and skip through the lanes hand-in-hand with your daughter. Be a child again for just a moment. Let some light back into your life.' Steve tried it. At first he felt foolish but soon he entered into the spirit of it and laughed out loud for all to hear. He began to feel alive once more. Something warm was entering his heart and bringing new-found health.

This is not offered as a complete list of the behavioural changes that a person may be required to make after suffering from burnout. It is, however, a working list of the most common needs, based on the experience of many burnout victims and their road to recovery.

Skill improvement

Lowering or avoiding negative stress should be our goal if we are to recover from or avoid burnout. For this we need improved skills. It is often assumed that the Christian ministry is the same role wherever it is carried out. This is a mistake and fails to take account of the differing needs of both church and minister. Some churches are looking for strategists, others for managers, pastors, evangelists, teachers, etc. Misplaced Christian ministers will experience heavy negative stresses, as will the churches with which they are misplaced.

Gifting

Many Christian ministers are fulfilling a pastoral role when they are evangelists, and others are required to be evangelists when they are in reality pastors. Denominations often have no provision for full-time Christian workers other than the pastoral ministry and so many enter the ministry without the appropriate gifting. This results in an increase of role pressure that may lead to burnout. There is no ready answer to this without radical denominational rethinking. However, increased self-awareness may help those who are seeking their next church. An awareness of one's gifting, strengths and weaknesses may help with placement as these things are openly discussed. There are tools, such as the Modified Houtts Questionnaire available from Fuller Seminary, Pasadena, USA, to help us measure our gifting. This and other tests help us to take an inventory of our gifting so that we may, where possible, do what we are good at and be free to be who we are. It is important to note that gifting may change with the years and a regular measurement of our gifts may help.

Case study

Timothy is a Baptist minister in his mid-fifties. He came into the ministry later in life, having been an architect since leaving college in his early twenties. Timothy was an excellent pastor when it came to visiting the sick and the elderly. He could bring them a sense of support, love and hope that was an enormous encouragement to many. However, he was not a good preacher or teacher and had never quite admitted this to himself.

The time came for him to move to another church and Timothy set his sights on a new church plant, believing he was the man God would use to lead them to growth. Timothy took up the post and before long found life becoming difficult. He could work well with the needy but was neither a strategist nor an evangelist; the very requirement of this church for its minister. Timothy left the church after a short time, a broken man, believing himself to be worthless, when in fact he was wrongly placed.

In his previous profession he would never have considered employing a plumber as an architect or a mechanic as a builder – it would have seemed foolish to him. And yet the role of the Christian minister is viewed as one role, when it is many. It changes from church to church in terms of what that church needs in the way of gifting at that time in their development.

Reflection

Consider the following statement: 'It is assumed that the Christian ministry is the same role wherever it is carried out. This is a mistake and fails to take account of the differing needs of both church and minister.'

Worth

A major stressor for the minister is to measure worth by results. The misplaced minister will agonise over this since his or her gifting is unable to be seen to be fruitful. Worth is something that God awards to all of humanity and is not indicated by results or giftedness. Christian ministers often live with a sense of failure because they have to do what they were not called to do. Increasingly this role carries with it managerial responsibility. In a recent survey many Christian ministers said that they lacked management training, but few of them attended or planned to attend any conferences or take any in-service training to address this need. Many are therefore working under conditions of great stress without a plan to alleviate this and suffer with feelings of worthlessness and failure.

Delegation

Many Christian ministers report that they lack the ability to undertake some of their regular tasks. They feel that they have not been trained sufficiently in certain areas. One way of overcoming this while increasing the feelings of value on the part of other people in the church is to learn to delegate aspects of the role. This can only be done comfortably if your security is found in who you are and not in what you do.

Case study

One large Congregational church in the USA invited an organisation involved in gifts and ministry measurement to test the entire leadership team, made up of three full-time ministers and eight lay-leaders.

The results were helpful and enabled them to divide up the necessary roles according to gifting without the senior minister feeling as if he were surplus to requirements. This required courage as the management of the church fell to a lay-leader who was an excellent manager. The senior pastor, who was a good teacher and leader, gave the pastoral responsibilities to others who were more gifted in this than he.

This all proved a great success and the church grew. Many church members reported that they enjoyed being in the church because they were encouraged to contribute to the overall plan.

Some Christian ministers admit to holding on to the various aspects of their work for fear that they will lose their place or give away their leadership. They often fear the involvement of others, because they cannot see what they would do if more gifted people were to take on roles.

Delegation can be highly freeing and can help a church to function better. It can also alleviate some of the high stress faced by ministers as the result of work overload.

Further training

Christian ministers and others in the caring professions need to feel free to admit that they are not trained in certain areas of work. Many courses exist that would help them to improve in their required roles, for example:

- Communication
- Teaching
- Management

- Self-management
- Counselling
- Writing
- Interpersonal skills
- Assertiveness
- Thinking
- Problem solving
- Conflict resolution

Case study

Timothy, from our story earlier, spent many long hours preparing teaching sermons for his congregation. It didn't matter how many hours he put in, the sermons didn't improve. He could not get across what he felt God had spoken to him. Timothy needed further training in Bible teaching if he was to continue in this role and he also needed to improve his communication skills.

Overcoming negative stress for healthy living may well include training for change. It is important that the sufferer from burnout be made to feel that this is a positive, building dimension and not a punishment for failure. A fresh attitude to specialist training needs to be adopted as an ongoing aspect of training ministers.

The future

Staying with change

Sufferers from burnout may have undergone some of the therapeutic processes outlined in this chapter of the book. They will have benefited from this, but in order to avoid burnout for the future many of the lessons learned need to be implemented as ongoing patterns of life. Burnout has resulted from poor patterns of working and these patterns must now be avoided completely.

Regular check-ups

Sufferers from burnout who have followed the suggestions made in this chapter will have made a professional relationship with a counsellor or therapist. I suggest that they plan to visit these professionals once every six months simply to talk over current issues and check their present condition. This is not suggested from the belief that some permanent weakness will stay with the former sufferer from burnout. Quite the contrary; former sufferers, having worked on their issues and working patterns, may now be in a better place for a healthy future. It is healthy to develop an ongoing plan for regular check-ups to avoid the build-up of unprocessed stresses.

Support groups

I have suggested the use of support groups to help the sufferer from burnout to recover. I further suggest that all serving ministers build support groups as an ongoing feature of their working lives. These are honest places for reflection and consideration, providing the individual with a secure environment. Also these support groups provide the serving minister with a system of accountability so often lacking from their lives.

Much of the discussion in this chapter revolves around lifestyle changes. Health is maintained by working with healthy patterns of life. Good diet, regular exercise, regular time off, etc. need to be maintained for their benefits to continue. Burnout is a painful and debilitating experience that may be avoided and can be healed, but not without an informed response that takes account of its seriousness.

Reflection

Write down any changes in your ministry or personal motif that you now consider require your attention if you are to remain healthy in your ministry. Look back through the book as you do this to remind yourself of those aspects that have touched you the most.

Conclusion

Those who have sensed that they have a calling or a vocation to serve God as ministers or leaders in His Church conduct the Christian ministry today. This calling may cause respondents to feel that their role in life is different from other caring roles. Since human beings cannot escape their humanity, ministers bring to their role an emotional history, a personality and a belief system that will affect the experience of the role.

This book suggests that these dynamics working together may cause ministers to develop an unrealistic set of expectations for their role, particularly if they embrace the servant role to the extent that they do not care sufficiently for their own health and well-being. Where this is the case, occupational stress results.

This book supports the view that many ministers are carrying heavy workloads and that they are often not sufficiently well-resourced to avoid suffering high levels of stress. Many overwork as they attempt to achieve the perceived expectations of the denomination, the local church, and their own view of the work of a minister. This means that there is significant risk that many ministers may become victims of the condition of burnout. When this happens many may be unable to work in their role for prolonged periods while they go through a process of recovery. The work here points to these conclusions: that healthy concepts of call and vocation, which include a balanced view of the humanity of the minister and a well-developed self-awareness, together with healthy views of the needs of human beings to sustain fulfilled productivity and healthy life and work boundaries, can lessen the negative stresses experienced by ministers and enable them to avoid the destructive nature of burnout. These boundaries would include the need for a positive support environment and a positive supervisory system to strengthen the levels of care experienced by ministers, as well as defined boundaries between work and rest, giving out and replenishing energy.

These health-giving dynamics represent an area of learning about self and the role of minister or Christian leader that may not currently be available in pre-ordination training. This book suggests that such a focus needs to be taken up in training establishments and by denominations at pre- or post-ordination levels, and possibly at both. It suggests that all

Christian leaders establish mature and health giving approaches to their adopted lifestyle in order to *be* their best, to *do* their best and *experience* the best, breathing life into the Church through the positive modelling of the Christian life.

Resources

Claybury International/The Claybury Trust

Email: Admin@Claybury.com
Website: www.claybury.org
International initiatives in the care and development of leaders through training, consulting, counselling.

One Another Ministries International

Email: Info@OneAnother.com
Website: www.oneanother.com
Training, consulting and counselling – providing tools Christian workers can use to make their lives and ministries more joyful and effective over the long-term.

Evangelical Alliance 'Care for Pastors Network'

website: www.careforpastors.org.uk
A gateway to UK resources available to Christian leaders via the Internet.

Churches' Ministerial Counselling Service

Email: admin@cmcs.org.uk
Website: www.cmcs.org.uk
A network of professional counsellors, operating in England, Scotland and Wales. It is sponsored by the Baptist Union of Great Britain, the Methodist Church, the Salvation Army, the United Reformed Church and the Free Churches Group of Churches together in England (acting on behalf of other Free Church denominations).

Liberating the Leadership Course

This course is available as part of the distance learning programme of the London School of Theology and is obtainable from and administered by the Open Learning Department. It will take you through similar material but will allow you to work at a deeper level and over a longer period of time. The course also provides you with college credits as part of your work for a possible diploma or degree through the open learning programme. For information contact the department on 01923 456230.Website: www.lst.ac.uk/open/

Notes

Introduction

1. C.D. Buckland, *Leaders Under Pressure* (London: Evangelical Alliance, 1996).

Chapter 4

1. E.B. Bratcher, *The Walk on Water Syndrome* (Waco: Word, 1984).
2. A.D. Hart, *Coping with Depression in the Ministry and Other Helping Professions* (Dallas: Word, 1984), p.19.
3. H.J.M. Nouwen, *The Genesee Diary* (New York: Image, 1981), p.84.
4. S.P. Daniel and M.L. Rogers, 'Burnout and the pastorate', *Journal of Psychology and Theology*, vol. 9:3 (1981), pp.232–249.
5. 'Gift-awareness' meaning the minister's awareness of particular strengths in ministry.
6. Bratcher, *Walk on Water Syndrome*, p.27.
7. H.J.M. Nouwen, *Intimacy: Essays in Pastoral Psychology* (Harper & Row, 1969), pp.5–22.

Chapter 7

1. L. McBurney, *Counselling Christian Workers* (Waco: Word, 1986), pp.35–36.
2. H.W. Schaumburg, *False Intimacy* (Colorado: NavPress, 1992).
3. 'Mentor–protégé' is a term that describes the relationship between the carer and the cared for.
4. P. Rutter, *Sex in the Forbidden Zone* (London: Mandala, 1991), p.11.
5. Center for the Prevention of Sexual and Domestic Violence, *Workshop Manual*, p.33.
6. Rutter, *Sex in the Forbidden Zone*, p.42.
7. Ibid, p.58.
8. 'He' because statistically the vast majority of sexual offenders are male.
9. Rutter, *Sex in the Forbidden Zone*, *op.cit.* pp.160–161.
10. 'Client' refers to anyone in the professional care of the minister.

Chapter 8

1. An anonymous monk, quoted by Rowland Croucher (ed.), *Still Waters, Deep Waters* (Albatross Books, 1987), pp.30–31.

Chapter 9

1. A.D. Hart, *The Hidden Link Between Adrenalin and Stress* (Nashville, Tennessee: Word Publishing, 1986), pp.37–38. All rights reserved.
2. H. Selye, *The Stress of Life*, quoted in Hart, *Adrenalin and Stress*, p.65.
3. M. Friedman and H. Rosenman, *Type-A Behavior and Your Heart* (New York: Knopf, 1974), p.178.
4. G. Davies, *Stress: The Challenge to Christian Caring* (Eastbourne: Kingsway Publications, 1988), p.61.
5. H. Freudenberger and G. Richelsen, *Burnout: The High Cost of High Achievement* (New York: Bantam, 1981), p.14.
6. A.M. Pines et al., *Burnout: From Tedium to Growth* (New York: The Free Press, 1981), p.17.
7. S. Fineman, *Social Work: Stress and Intervention* (Aldershot: Gower, 1985), p.57.
8. M. Rush, *Burnout* (Amersham: Scripture Press, 1989), p.13.
9. J. Sanford, *Ministry Burnout* (Hemel Hempstead: Arthur James, 1984), p.3.
10. E.W. McCormick, *Breakdown* (Berkeley: Optima, 1993), p.6.
11. L. McBurney, *Counselling Christian Workers* (Waco: Word, 1986), p.178.
12. Rush, *Burnout*, op. cit. p.60.
13. B. Fletcher, *Clergy Under Stress* (London: Mowbray, 1990), p.1.
14. H.W. Schaumburg, *False Intimacy* (Colorado Springs: NavPress, 1992), pp.11–29.

Chapter 10

1. M.A. Coate, *Clergy Stress* (London: SPCK, 1989), p.112.
2. B. Fletcher, *Clergy Under Stress* (London: Mowbray, 1990), p.43.
3. L. McBurney, *Counselling Christian Workers* (Waco: Word, 1986), p.179.
4. Coate, *Clergy Stress*, op. cit. p.194.
5. Ibid, p.8.
6. Ibid, p.8.
7. Ibid, p.73.
8. Fletcher, *Clergy Under Stress*, op. cit. p.34.
9. A.D. Hart, *Coping with Depression in the Ministry and Other Helping Professions* (Dallas: Word, 1984), p.118.
10. Fletcher, *Clergy Under Stress*, op. cit. p.26.
11. Ibid, p.26.

National Distributors

UK: (and countries not listed below)
CWR, Waverley Abbey House, Waverley Lane, Farnham, Surrey GU9 8EP.
Tel: (01252) 784700 Outside UK +44 1252 784700

AUSTRALIA: CMC Australasia, PO Box 519, Belmont, Victoria 3216.
Tel: (03) 5241 3288 Fax: (03) 5241 3290

CANADA: Cook Communications Ministries, PO Box 98, 55 Woodslee Avenue, Paris, Ontario N3L 3E5. Tel: 1800 263 2664

GHANA: Challenge Enterprises of Ghana, PO Box 5723, Accra.
Tel: (021) 222437/223249 Fax: (021) 226227

HONG KONG: Cross Communications Ltd, 1/F, 562A Nathan Road, Kowloon.
Tel: 2780 1188 Fax: 2770 6229

INDIA: Crystal Communications, 10-3-18/4/1, East Marredpalli, Secunderabad – 500026, Andhra Pradesh Tel/Fax: (040) 27737145

KENYA: Keswick Books and Gifts Ltd, PO Box 10242, Nairobi.
Tel: (02) 331692/226047 Fax: (02) 728557

MALAYSIA: Salvation Book Centre (M) Sdn Bhd, 23 Jalan SS 2/64, 47300 Petaling Jaya, Selangor.
Tel: (03) 78766411/78766797 Fax: (03) 78757066/78756360

NEW ZEALAND: CMC Australasia, PO Box 36015, Lower Hutt.
Tel: 0800 449 408 Fax: 0800 449 049

NIGERIA: FBFM, Helen Baugh House, 96 St Finbarr's College Road, Akoka, Lagos.
Tel: (01) 7747429/4700218/825775/827264

PHILIPPINES: OMF Literature Inc, 776 Boni Avenue, Mandaluyong City.
Tel: (02) 531 2183 Fax: (02) 531 1960

SINGAPORE: Armour Publishing Pte Ltd, Block 203A Henderson Road, 11-06 Henderson Industrial Park, Singapore 159546.
Tel: 6 276 9976 Fax: 6 276 7564

SOUTH AFRICA: Struik Christian Books, 80 MacKenzie Street, PO Box 1144, Cape Town 8000.
Tel: (021) 462 4360 Fax: (021) 461 3612

SRI LANKA: Christombu Publications (Pvt) Ltd., Bartleet House, 65 Braybrooke Place, Colombo 2.
Tel: (01) 433142/328909

TANZANIA: CLC Christian Book Centre, PO Box 1384, Mkwepu Street, Dar es Salaam.
Tel/Fax: (022) 2119439

USA: Cook Communications Ministries, PO Box 98, 55 Woodslee Avenue, Paris, Ontario N3L 3E5, Canada. Tel: 1800 263 2664

ZIMBABWE: Word of Life Books (Pvt) Ltd, Christian Media Centre, 8 Aberdeen Road, Avondale, PO Box A480 Avondale, Harare, Zimbabwe Tel: (04) 333355 or 091301188

For email addresses, visit the CWR website: www.cwr.org.uk

CWR is a registered charity – Number 294387

CWR is a limited company registered in England – Registration Number 1990308